FREDERICK D. BUGGIE

NEW
PRODUCT
DEVELOPMENT
STRATEGIES

A DIVISION OF AMERICAN MANAGEMENT ASSOCIATIONS

Library of Congress Cataloging in Publication Data

Buggie, Frederick D.
  New product development strategies.

    Bibliography: p.
    Includes index.
    1. New products. I. Title.
HD69.N4B825   658.5'75   81-66230
ISBN 0-8144-5626-X   AACR2

© 1981 AMACOM
A division of American Management Associations, New York.
All rights reserved. Printed in the United States of America.

First Printing

NEW PRODUCT DEVELOPMENT STRATEGIES

ACKNOWLEDGMENT

I wish to acknowledge the unflagging support and confidence demonstrated by Robert R. Steigerwald, Vice President of Strategic Innovations, Inc., who participated in the development of many of the strategies described in this book.

CONTENTS

PART THREE
IMPLEMENTING ACTION

PART ONE

CREATIVITY
IN
BUSINESS

1

INNOVATION
IN
CONTEXT

For a business—any business—to prosper in the long run, it must be managed by people who possess both *acumen* and *creativity*. By acumen I mean the ability to make quick, accurate judgments; by creativity I mean the ability to generate new options. Both abilities need to be brought to bear on tasks of the corporation. One without the other will not do, or the business will atrophy in the long run.

The problem is that "acumen" is generally taught (in business schools), practiced (in business), and rewarded (by the company), whereas "creativity" is generally not taught, not practiced, not rewarded. The result is that most organizations—especially old, large, successful-up-to-now organizations—possess more acumen than they need, and less creativity than they need, to sustain their growth and prosperity. In fact, in many ways the modern corporation seems to be designed to *prevent* creativity. And the modern socialization process appears to be designed to stifle everyone's inherent creativity.

"RESPECTED AUTHORITIES"

First, let's look at the individual. Consider the typical successful business executive, the eminent scientist, the noted engineer—the "authority in his field." As he matures and benefits from experience, he becomes increasingly competent. His wisdom increases. His judgment improves. His decisions gain a reputation for reliability. He is consistent, stable, dependable. Few mistakes. No surprises. If you plotted his wisdom and judgment (acumen) against his "maturity" on the horizontal axis, you would get a straight northeast line.

If you use "education and training" for the horizontal axis, instead of "maturity," and plot wisdom/judgment against it, the relationship is the same. The lines look a lot alike—a linear, positive correlation in each case. The prominent executive—the noted authority—is an expert in his field.

At the same time, however, he may gradually develop some degree of tunnel vision—or to use Thorstein Veblen's term, "educated incapacity." Steeped in his particular area of wisdom, he is unable to appreciate the significance of knowledge in fields outside his own. As Abraham Maslow, the motivational psychologist, so succinctly put it: if the only tool you have is a hammer, you will treat everything you come in contact with as if it were a nail.

As a result of this narrow focus, the judgments made by "noted authorities" may not always be sustainable. In fact, they may ultimately be proved wrong. For example:

◇ In 1945 Admiral Halsey told President Truman that an atomic bomb was infeasible. It could never be detonated. And he spoke as an expert on explosives.
◇ Thomas Edison thought Charles Steinmetz was on the wrong track in fooling with alternating current. To Edison, direct current was the only way to go.
◇ Detroit Edison Co. offered young Henry Ford a job, pro-

vided he stop tinkering with the internal combustion engine.

◇ In 1940 our National Academy of Sciences issued a statement declaring that there would never be such a thing as jet aircraft: "Even considering the improvements possible—the gas turbine could hardly be considered a feasible application to airplanes, mainly because of the difficulty of complying with the stringent weight requirements." (Who on earth are we to believe, if not the National Academy of Sciences?)

◇ Finally, remember that the world hasn't been round for very long—only 500 years. Before that it was flat for a long, long time.

The point is that respected authorities, and in fact the body of public opinion, may be dead wrong. Irrefutable truths and universal assumptions are open to challenge. But who is to challenge them? It is awfully difficult to do so in an autocratic organization, where precedence is revered and deference is accorded to those in charge. It is equally difficult to march to the beat of a different drummer in a democratic environment where great premium is placed on being "one of the guys."

THE SOCIALIZATION PROCESS

I once talked with a group of Japanese business executives about apparent differences exhibited in our two cultures with respect to innovation. They suggested that the cause may lie in our differing socialization processes. In Japan, children are brought up under a very strict regimen and are taught rigid adherence to the mores of the family and the culture. Having internalized the need for approval in childhood, Japanese adults then have the confidence to depart from the norm. In America, by contrast—at least according to the theory advanced by these Japanese executives—children are disciplined inconsistently and

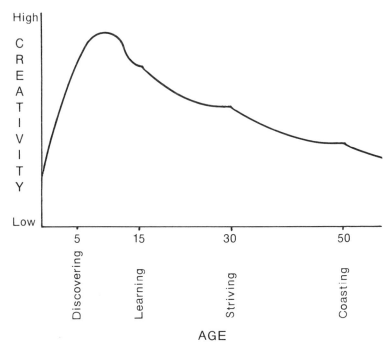

Figure 1. Creativity versus age.

haphazardly and therefore continue into adulthood craving the approbation of others. This continuing need for approval stifles creativity and fosters conformity.

Let's examine the socialization process as it affects the natural creativity that every child possesses. As Sid Shore, editor of *Creativity in Action*, points out, we were all children once. In the beginning, we exhibit a healthy curiosity. We try out whatever appeals to us. We fit different things together. We don't know enough not to do some pretty peculiar things. Then we start going to school, and the process of socialization begins. We learn a lot. We get a job. We get along. We coast.

Several years ago, Dr. John Bujake, who is now a vice president of the 7-Up Company, conducted a study of the degradation of creativity as a function of maturity. In his words, "By the time they're six, they're ruined!" Every study I have seen confirms that same general conclusion: the creativity exhibited by the average person decreases with age and education. (See Figure 1.)

It must be emphasized that all the foregoing applies to the *average* person, under *normal* conditions. This is not to say that some exceptional people do not escape these forces. And it certainly does not imply that any of us has to settle for "normal" conditions. All of us can tap the latent creativity we possess. It's simply a matter of knowing what to do, and practicing it (as with any learnable skill, from playing racquetball to strumming the banjo).

CREATIVITY DEFINED

What is creativity? Maybe this story will give us an idea of what we are talking about.

A motorist was driving past an insane asylum when suddenly he had a blowout. He managed to bring his car under control and parked at the curb beside the steel fence, where one of the inmates was strolling. The driver got out and started changing his flat tire. He jacked up the car, removed the lug nuts, removed the flat, and put on the spare tire. Then he inadvertently tipped over the wheelcover in which he had placed the lug nuts, sending them rolling down the sewer drain. The inmate of the asylum observed with interest. The driver mumbled to himself, "What am I going to do? How can I drive my car on only three wheels?" The inmate spoke up: "Why don't you remove two lug nuts from each of the other wheels and use them to secure that wheel?"

"What a great idea!" exclaimed the driver. "But how did you think of that? You're supposed to be crazy."

To which the inmate replied: "I may be crazy, but I'm not stupid!" (For "not stupid" read "not lacking in creativity.")

Everybody has his own favorite definition of creativity. Here are a few:

◇ "Creativity is the production of meaning by synthesis." (Dr. Myron S. Allen)

◇ "The ability to relate and connect, sometimes in odd and yet striking fashion, lies at the very heart of any creative use of the mind, no matter in what field or discipline." (George J. Seidel)

◇ "It is obvious that invention or discovery, be it in mathematics or anywhere else, takes place by combining ideas." (Jacques Hadamard)

◇ "Creativity is a marvelous capacity to grasp two mutually distinct realities, without going beyond the field of our experience, and to draw a spark from their juxtaposition." (Anonymous)

Dr. Frederic Flach, clinical associate professor of psychiatry at Cornell University Medical College, credits L. S. Kubie with the observation that, at the preconscious level, we can "rapidly mobilize large quantities of data and superimpose dissimilar ingredients into new . . . conceptual patterns, 'reshuffling experiences to achieve those fantastic degrees of condensation, without which creativity in any field of activity would be impossible.' " According to this view, an individual must "disorganize and reorganize his thinking" in order to come up with new concepts. Arthur Koestler, in his book *The Act of Creation*, calls the process *reculer pour mieux sauter*, or taking a step backward in order to make a leap forward.

In his book *Creativity and Innovation*, John Haefele offers this formula to define creativity:

$$A + B \rightarrow C$$

where A is a known element, B is a known element, and the arrow represents the insight to link them together in an innovative way, yielding C, a new compound. C then may become an element of another new compound. And so invention, and the technology on which invention is based, proliferates. An example of this phenomenon:

Thermometer + Bimetal + Mercury Switch → Thermostat

And then:

Thermostat + Clock → Automatic Thermostat

And then:

Automatic Thermostat + Semiconductor →
Automated Actuator

Or a more down-to-earth example:

Shaft + Motor + String → Weed-Eater®

THE CREATIVE PERSONALITY

How can you identify creative people? What sort of characteristics do they possess? Here are some descriptions given by participants in workshops and seminars on applying innovation to business goals. Creative people are:

Curious	Resourceful
Imaginative	Imprecise
Self-confident	Intelligent
Open-minded	Responsive
Able to concentrate	Independent
Persistent	Energetic
Adventurous	Unconventional
Sensitive	Compulsive
Skeptical	Unpredictable

If these adjectives smack to you of the Boy Scout oath, you can use less flattering words—egotistical, flighty, nonconforming, inaccurate, peculiar, difficult to manage, and so on—but you get to the same place. Creative people are different and don't mind being different.

Psychiatrists have made numerous studies of creative people over the past 25 years. The results very much confirm the impressions of seminar participants. Dallas and Gaier, in "Identification of Creativity: The Individual" (*The Psychology Bulletin*, 1970), reported that creative people commonly reveal high self-reliance and independence. They are intuitive, flexible, and open to stimuli; they have a wide variety of interests and are unconcerned about social norms. They are introspective, socially detached, fond of challenges, egotistical, resilient, and assertive. Creative people accomplish more work than others in a shorter period of time. D. W. MacKinnon, in "Personality and the Realization of Creative Potential" (*American Psychology*, 1965), reported that creative people are able to tolerate ambiguities without needing the kind of certainty that more "compulsively organized" people often require.

Now, having covered what creativity is and what a creative person is like, let's put A and B together. What is the yield? The bottom line is: *creative people generate lots of new ideas, ideas that are new to them.*

The fact that the concept already exists somewhere or that somebody else already thought of it is irrelevant. The second inventor is just as creative as the first; it's simply a matter of timing. I'm beginning to believe there is such a thing as a time for which an idea comes, as well as the reverse. The quantitative aspect is significant: creative people generate *many* new ideas. The person who comes up with one "big hit" may not be especially creative, just as the golfer who birdies a hole once may be lucky rather than talented. The qualitative aspect is significantly absent: creative people generate ideas without passing judgment on them. The alleged value of a new concept has nothing to do with creativity. "Value" is simply a subsequent judgment passed by society, or by the organization. Moreover, as we have already seen, the assessments rendered on new ideas are not infallible.

Now the bottom line for any organization is that it must attract *some* creative people, it must encourage the practice of *some* creativity, and it must reward effort as well as success if it is to survive in the long run.

2

OBSTACLES
TO
CREATIVITY

Fortunately, creativity—the ability to generate new options—is indeed inherent in all of us, to a greater or lesser extent. The ability may be latent (understandably) but it's there. And the first step to "accessing" that skill, for application to practical business tasks, is to recognize the hindrances to creativity that the typical corporate executive faces. There are twelve fundamental hindrances to creativity—six "built in" to the individual, and six imposed on the individual by the corporation. Six of one, half a dozen of the other.

PERSONAL HINDRANCES

1. *The bicamerality of the brain.* Scientific research indicates that the brain is composed of two hemispheres, each with distinctly different functions. In the normal, mature, right-handed male, the left hemisphere of the brain controls logical, analytical, propositional thought, while the right hemisphere is reserved for conceptual, holistic, appositional thought.

The left side is totally organized. That's where we build categories and classify everything we perceive. We round off edges and fill in blanks (psychologists call it "closure") so that anything new we see is indexed and classified with a group of somehow similar things we have seen before. That's also where the written word resides. It's a tidy world.

The right hemisphere is totally unorganized. That's where music, art, poetry, vague "feelings," intuition, and the voices of the gods are heard. It's a strange world.

The essence of creativity is using the right side of your brain to combine known elements into new or different relationships. If you immediately put everything you see into a little cubbyhole in the left side of your brain, you will have precious little opportunity to develop new combinations.

2. *Conservation of energy.* Successful solutions tend to be repeated. When you face a new situation or problem, you engage in search-and-try activity until a satisfactory solution is found. It may not be the best solution, but it gets the job done. When you again face that (almost) identical situation, it is no longer a problem—you pull out your old solution and, sure enough, it works again. Pretty soon, after a little practice, and uniformly good results (positive reinforcement), the habit becomes ingrained and you go on "automatic pilot." You perform that procedure by rote, paying no attention to the matter whatsoever. Why should you?

You're quite right—you've got better, more important things to command your attention. But if you are not really perceiving the "known elements," you have nothing to work with in developing new combinations. Creativity never has a chance if you think you "know all about" the problem.

That is a mental manifestation of the "conservation of energy" hindrance. There is a physical manifestation as well: a body at rest tends to remain at rest—and I mean a *body*. Creative activity is hard work. The brain is fueled by oxygen and glucose carried by blood as the vehicle. The amount of oxygen and glucose reaching the brain during any interval of time is determined by pressure, which is increased or decreased as a function of physical activity. So the slothful slouch will not get very high horsepower out of his creativity machine.

3. *Adherence to convention.* When I was a little boy, I asked my father if it was good manners to do this or that at table, and he replied, "After you learn the basics, you can properly do anything that is not conspicuous." Adhering to convention, following precedent, staying in line—all these things are trained in us from childhood as good ways to avoid criticism and punishment. Later, we receive gratification of some of our social needs (which Maslow has identified for us) by being one of the gang, "fitting in," hewing to the party line. If you never venture afield, never try something new, you'll never do anything creative.

4. *Fear of the unknown.* The words "foreign" and "alien" have secondary, negative connotations in our own and in other languages. We are comfortable and confident with the known, the familiar. The strange, the different, the unusual, and the new are "exciting" at best. They are more often fearsome. We haven't been down that track before and we don't know what to expect. The light at the end of the tunnel may be an approaching train. It's much safer and easier to stay with the good old friendly, familiar way.

5. *The wandering mind.* A well-known Columbia University study showed that 83 per cent of all our new knowledge comes to our brain via our eyes and 11 per cent via our ears. We read at about 300 words per minute, and we listen to normal speech at around 125 words per minute. Yet the brain has the capacity to receive 27 "bits" of information per second. So when we're reading or supposedly listening, often we aren't at all. We're thinking about something totally unrelated. We check back in once in a while, and then out of sheer boredom we go off to other, more interesting diversions. The brain is perverse. Attention is very

difficult to channel and control. We may believe we're working on a problem, trying to come up with a creative solution, when in reality often we are not.

6. *Paranoia.* Some especially creative people who make their living by coming up with new ideas—advertising people, inventors, architects, corporate strategists, R&D engineers—have fallen prey to a Dr. Hook or two among their associates. They have seen some of their ideas appropriated by others with impunity, and then developed, promoted, and capitalized on by these pretenders. They have seen the rewards for innovation—both psychic and financial—go to these pirates, while they toil away in obscurity.

And those truly creative people may be right. There is a pithy apothegm: "I may be paranoid, but that doesn't mean they're not out to get me!" If creative people have repeated experiences of this kind, they may stop creating, or stop expressing their ideas to anybody. That is the ultimate preventive against piracy.*

You can do something about each of the personal hindrances to creativity yourself. As Pogo said, "We have met the enemy— and they are us." And top management of the company can do something about the following hindrances imposed on the individual by the corporation.

CORPORATE HINDRANCES

1. *The price of being wrong.* In some companies an executive gets only one chance to make a mistake, a big mistake for which he is clearly and solely responsible. Other companies are more tolerant. But in no organization is it beneficial to one's career to fail frequently. Therefore, the safest course for the executive, by all odds, is to keep on keepin' on—do things in accordance with

---

* My thanks to C. W. Axelrod of Great Neck, New York, for help in identifying this last personal hindrance to creativity. Actually, he just expressed the idea succinctly. I had, myself, observed this same syndrome previously!

standard practice, according to policy, and take no chances. The surest way to avoid mistakes is not to try anything you haven't successfully done before—the risks are too great.

2. *The need for justification.* All organizations number among their members guardians of the present order. Anything new is viewed with suspicion. A new idea could change priorities, cost money, diminish responsibility, dilute effort—or a hundred other corporate disasters. These friendly keepers of the status quo generally preface their criticism with "I'm just playing devil's advocate, you understand," and proceed to devastate your fledgling idea. The result is that the concept is dismissed out of hand before it gets a real chance. It has been so for almost 500 years, as exemplified by this assertion by Machiavelli:

> It must be considered that there is nothing more difficult to carry out, nor more doubtful of success, nor dangerous to handle, than to initiate a new order of things. For the reformer has enemies in all those who profit by the old order, and only lukewarm defenders in all those who would profit by the new order, this lukewarmness arising partly from fear of their adversaries, who have the laws in their favor; and partly from the incredulity of mankind, who do not truly believe in anything new until they have had actual experience of it. Thus it arises that on every opportunity for attacking the reformer, his opponents do so with the zeal of partisans, the others only defend him half-heartedly, so that between them he runs great danger.

3. *Vested reputation.* When an executive makes his mark— when he does hit a big winner—what incentive does he have to try anything .new again? He can hit again, in which case he's about where he was—or he can come a cropper (and the odds are that he will), in which case his reputation as a creative genius becomes somewhat tarnished. So he is in a no-win situation and the best thing he can do is tuck in his neck and rest on his laurels. One big success can ruin a creative contributor. Of course, that is not always the case. Some people are incorrigible inquirers; they simply ignore the end results of their creative probing and continue to come up with new possibilities.

4. *Pressure to produce.* The folkways of business demand that employees give the appearance of being "earnestly engaged" at all times during working hours. That is, they should give some evidence of motion, or at least consciousness, and consistently exhibit "seriousness of purpose." That all relates to the *process* of business. With respect to the *results* of business, there is some presumption on the part of the corporation that there will be some measurable outcome from this activity after a period of time—a presumption that on its face does not seem unreasonable. The employee himself feels a need to see something accomplished after a hard day's work. (Maslow calls it "self-actualization.")

But here's the rub. In the first place, when someone is truly engaged in strenuous creativity, he may show no outward signs of life and, furthermore, he may adopt a most unbusinesslike posture or situate himself in a very unworklike station.

And secondly, there may well be no physical traces of his hard work—nothing to show for all that creative effort. Yet the new concept he has generated may revolutionize a process, create a whole new product line, or reorganize the company.

On the other hand, he may just be goofing off. You can't tell from outside.

5. *Overmanagement.* In order to have the opportunity to work at creativity, the worker must be left to his own devices. Yet between responsibilities assigned, schedules and deadlines to be met, the organizing and supervision of teams and individual workers (plain meddling), and miscellaneous irrelevant distractions, the executive often has little opportunity for creativity. There is simply no time to spend contemplating possible new approaches to problems. The only safe course is to follow the thoroughly predictable procedure that has proved adequate in the past. You're locked in.

6. *Frustration forecast.* Even if an executive has the opportunity to generate truly creative solutions—and possesses the temerity (foolhardiness) to do so—he may refrain from the effort

because he has been conditioned by the corporation not to bother. Many companies simply do not respond at any level to the stimulus of a creative proposal. It's a bit like throwing a rock into a tar pit—no ripples, no bubbles, nothing at all. It just sinks out of sight. After a few experiences of that sort, the innovative executive may rightly conclude that he should devote his energies to activities that will have greater impact on the organization and result in more tangible benefits.

At first blush, these dozen built-in hindrances to creativity may seem overwhelming. But I can assure you that, as the following chapters will show, all of them can be overcome.

3

OVERCOMING THE OBSTACLES, OR HOW TO BE MORE LIKE A RACCOON

Raccoons are quite creative in getting what they want. Empirical evidence abounds. Just open up the subject of the exploits of raccoons at any cocktail party on Gibson Island, Maryland, for example. You will hear all kinds of tales—eyewitness reports of one raccoon standing on the shoulders of another to reach the top of a garbage can, and similar exploits to achieve their goals.

Other animals, too, exhibit humanoid cleverness. Clinical experiments have shown that monkeys possess creative ability. In one instance they were observed dipping clams in the surf in order to rinse off the sand before eating them. Easy, you say? Pretty good if you're a monkey!

Any animal with a sufficient number of brain cells has the capacity to be creative. Man has 10 billion brain cells—far more than he needs to be creative. But man alone among animals commonly elects to restrict the uses of creativity to solve problems. The handicap is a matter of choice by default. If a person wants to slough off this handicap and avail himself of the additional working tool—creativity—he can do so by following some simple rules.

RULE 1: Necessity Is the Mother

There has to be some incentive, a strong incentive, to stimulate people to innovate or create. For the raccoon, the incentive of accessible food is enough motivation to get the trash can lid off.

RULE 2: Be Positive

You've got to have a positive, optimistic attitude. You can't be a grump and believe that no good can ever come from anything different or new. You've got to believe that improvements are possible. Man is the only animal with the ability to smile.

RULE 3: Collect Relevant New Data

With a little creativity you *can* turn a sow's ear into a silk purse—but you've got to have the sow's ear to start with. You can't make something from nothing. So begin not by trying to find a shortcut—a lucky hit to the answer—but by packing relevant raw materials to work with in your brain.

RULE 4: Change Your Perception

If you look at a problem from the same perspective that you have always looked at the problem, you're going to come up with the same old answers, and roadblocks. So the solution is, first, don't look at the "whole problem"—break it into separate parts and pieces—and, second, find some way to really see (perhaps for the first time) those elements of the whole. The classic creative techniques are useful for doing that. (See Chapter 12.)

RULE 5: Think in Sequence, Not in Parallel

If you start evaluating your ideas—whether they are good or bad, whether your second idea is better than your first, whether an idea is good enough to do the job that you're trying to do—you will soon bog down and prevent yourself from coming up with new "qualified" ideas. The barriers to entry to the club will be too high to let in a new member. So think wholly creatively first, accepting all ideas that come to you without eliminating anything. Only then, after you have all the bits and pieces on the table, sort out the good ones. Incidentally, during this judgmental/analytical phase, you may find it possible to refine, combine, and improve the original seed ideas.

RULE 6: Tolerate Ambiguity

The French mathematician and philosopher Poincaré said, "Disorder is the condition of the mind's fertility." Don't try to organize your thoughts or control your mind's meanderings: that's the job of the left side of your brain. It is the right side of the brain that is active in appositional, nonanalytic thought. You must withstand a bout of random fishing and searching without demanding the safe harbor of a "settled matter."

RULE 7: Work at It

As with any tough job, to achieve results you've got to try hard. Using creativity, like using a shovel, is not a dilettante's dalliance. You must persevere.

RULE 8: Eliminate Distractions

Generating new ideas requires uninterrupted concentration. Otherwise you may think you're thinking about the subject when you're actually musing about the interference. It's essential that you get away from your telephone and your in-box and those appealing "little" jobs.

RULE 9: Look for 100 Ways, Not the Answer

Assuming that you have selected an open-ended problem— one that will admit of more than one adequate solution— recognize that there are a number of acceptable "right" answers as well as an infinite number of wrong answers. Generate as many "possible" answers as you can. The larger your pool of possibilities, the more likely that a winner (or two) will be among them.

RULE 10: Verbalize

Words are the tools of thought. Don't underestimate the value of words as stimuli of creativity. Your brain bone may be connected to your tongue bone—in which case, start talking. Or your brain bone may be connected to your finger bone—in which case, start writing. But don't just stare at the problem.

RULE 11: Don't Trust Your Memory

The high rate of deterioration of the ability to recall has been scientifically proved. New ideas are ephemeral. Record them in some way before they are lost irretrievably. Ideas do not have the courtesy to announce themselves in advance and then arrive when expected, so be ready to trap them whenever they show up.

RULE 12: Let Up—Gestate

After you have focused on the task over a period of time until you are about used up, leave off! Go to something else—rest, play, sleep. Your subconscious will take over and continue the probe-and-search operation automatically.

RULE 13: Iterate

After a period of gestation, come back to the problem afresh. Your subconscious will then donate its contributions. Once you have judged the "pieces and parts," select the good ideas and concentrate only on them. Use them as raw materials, or points of departure for another creative climb from your new plateau. Finally, practice. As with any skill, the more you do it, the better you get.

RULE 14: Quit

There will come a point when additional creative effort becomes marginally productive. After you have done a workman-like job, don't continue seeking the holy grail. The task is complete. Take the best products of your effort—the best solutions—and *implement* them.

RULE 15: Don't Follow Rules

Bad ideas as well as good ideas follow rules. Loosen up. Smash a few icons. Do it *your* way, whatever way works. Everybody's different.

4

NEW-PRODUCT CONCEPTION

THE PRODUCT LIFE CYCLE

A few years ago, a man named Jones graphically depicted the metamorphosis of a product in the marketplace. His concept has since been recognized as the standard by professionals in the field of new-product conception and marketing strategy innovation.

The product-life-cycle curve, as it's called, applies across the board to any product line, any industry, any market. (See Figure 2.) The graph simply shows that a new product, upon introduction, starts from nothing, enters into a period of accelerating growth in revenues (impelled by the purchases of "pioneers" and "early adopters"), comes to a point of inflection in the curve when sales grow at a constant and then decreasing rate, and finally, begins to level off in sales.

Beyond that point, who knows? Your new product could meet a sudden demise, like the Hula Hoop and the Nehru jacket—a precipitous decline! Or it could follow Jell-O or Shredded Wheat (which was first introduced on March 1, 1893) and have a fairly

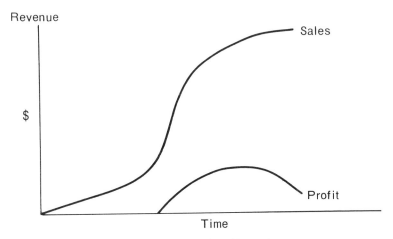

Figure 2. The product life cycle.

constant rate of continuing sales at a level somewhat below its initial peak. Ovaltine is forever! Or the life cycle of your product line could follow that of the Duncan Company—which looks a lot like a Yo-Yo over the long run.

I was in Santa Monica a while ago and saw that street skates had caught on with the young people. I was in Marina Del Rey even more recently and saw a number of *adults* roller-skating down the sidewalk. Who's going to bet on when street skates reach Kansas City, and how long the fad will last? (A lot of opportunistic, profit-motivated entrepreneurs, that's who!)

Notwithstanding the best efforts of market researchers and corporate planners, the dollar level of sales and the longevity of any new product are pretty hard to predict. New products introduced by any one firm tend to atrophy—their profit contribution disappears over time. The fad passes. You're eaten up by new competitors. The market becomes saturated. Technology moves on. (Roller-skate wheels have gone from metal to wood to plastic—is rubber next?)

The *typical* rate of product obsolescence varies from industry to industry. It is extraordinarily high in the electronics industry.

Toys and games live from Christmas to Christmas. Ten years ago product life cycles for new foods averaged two to three years; now they're down to about six months. On the other hand, the typical product life cycle in the machine tool industry is relatively sluggish. Numerically controlled machines are the first major innovation in that industry in a hundred years.

But it's not safe to go by averages and "industry" performance. The life cycles for individual products, within an industry, exhibit greater variations than the difference *among* industries. Guitars are different from pianos (and so are the companies that make them). We've already mentioned Shredded Wheat. Monopoly is a monopoly. The chairman of Warner & Swasey told me a few months ago that he noticed that one out of every five trucks backed up to his shipping platform was loaded with products that did not exist five years ago!

If you extrapolate the past product-life-cycle experience of your industry, company, or individual product line into the future, you will realize that you need to get cracking now on bringing new products on stream to supplant the income that will no longer be generated by your current products—"sooner or later."

That's just to stay even! Now, if a *growth* imperative is imposed, in the face of the inevitable attrition resulting from the product life cycle, you face a real crisis.

The "crisis" caused by the product life cycle combined with the growth required by management (and stockholders) is compounded by the current rate of inflation in our economy. What company is satisfied with 4 percent simple annual growth in the face of 12 percent compound inflation?

The Chinese word for "crisis" looks like this:

The left half means danger:

And the right half stands for opportunity:

Taking advantage of the opportunity inherent in a crisis is the essence of creative problem solving.

Successful new-product development is the solution to the crisis we're talking about here. That's fine! But which particular "new products" are you going to develop? How many of these ideas will succeed? What proportion will be launched in the marketplace—and, of them, what percentage will ultimately return a profit and enjoy any life cycle at all? What does the record show?

SUCCESS RATES—AND FAILURES

A couple of years ago, *The Journal of Marketing* reported:

> To produce a single successful new product, 80 ideas are required; seven-eighths of scientists' and engineers' development time is spent on products failing in introduction. Of every ten products that emerge from R&D, half fail in product and market tests, and only two become commercial successes.

Bert Cross, former chairman of the 3M Company, commented that in his company "out of every 100 new-product concepts, 33 will prove technically feasible; and of these 3 will become commercially successful in the market." In another firm's experience, "only 2 out of 58 new-product concepts ultimately succeed."

Is your company's success rate better than 3 to 5 percent? The rest of the world's record is not that good!

If this sort of situation is what can reasonably be expected, and you recognize that your firm does need an additional new product line, then your instant reaction might be to rush out and collect at least 50 new-product ideas to be sure of getting one that would have commercial success. Such a brute-force approach is impractical. To prove that, let's extrapolate back in time, from the starting point of our product-life-cycle curve.

From the instant a new-product idea is proposed, development effort and money begin to be spent on it. (See Figure 3.) Small

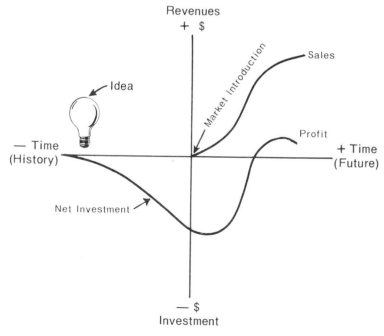

Figure 3. The product development cycle.

amounts at first—maybe just a drawing or concept statement. Then models, engineering drawings, market research, bench tests, redesign, pilot production, market testing. Investments increase incrementally as each benchmark is passed, and as favorable evaluations of the project are made by management along the way.

The money and development effort expended on products that are *scrubbed* somewhere along the line are totally wasted. And lots of these new-product concepts that survive the entire process

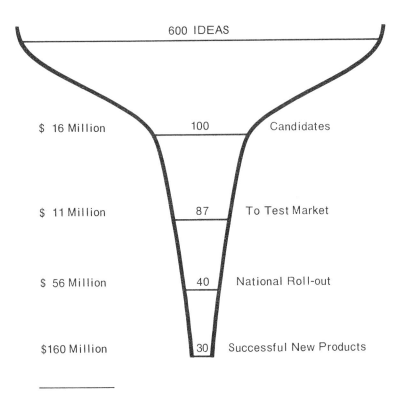

600 IDEAS

$ 16 Million   100   Candidates

$ 11 Million   87   To Test Market

$ 56 Million   40   National Roll-out

$160 Million   30   Successful New Products

$243 million — and 10 years!

Figure 4. The new-product "funnel" at General Foods.

still fail at the end of the line (market introduction) after the really big investments are made.

The graph in Figure 3 depicts only the successful new products. It does not take into account the 95 percent that are aborted along the way. The earlier you kill those new products destined to fail, the more money and development effort you will save, especially since the largest amounts are required toward the later stages. It costs the same to develop a failure as it does to develop a success.

Better yet: develop only the *successful* new-product ideas! But that's not possible, because the rousing successes and the turkeys look a lot alike during their early stages of development.

Figure 4 shows General Foods' experience in new-product development in a "typical" ten-year period, and they're pros at it!

THE "PERFECT" NEW PRODUCT

To improve the process of new-product development, perhaps the new-product *idea* is not the place to start! Perhaps it's better to lay some groundwork first—drawing up the "specifications" of the ideal new product abstractly—and then, take the initiative in generating new-product concepts to conform to the "specs."

The specifications, or criteria, for the "perfect new product" can be developed by establishing the minimum objectives it must meet and analyzing the strengths of your company that can be brought to bear on meeting those objectives. Figure 5 is a useful tool in formulating these criteria. It shows the directions your company can take in developing new products, depending on your unique capabilities.

Of all possible markets that could be served, your company is a strong factor in certain segments. In those segments your current products are known; you enjoy an established reputation; you "know your way around."

Of all possible technologies and manufacturing capabilities, your company is knowledgeable and experienced in certain pro-

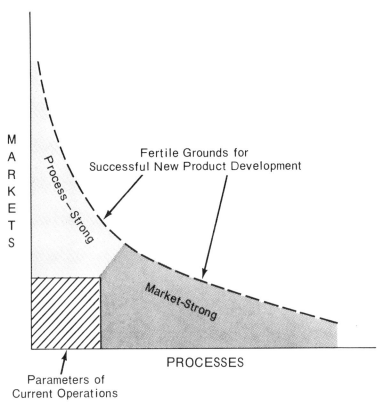

Figure 5. Broad direction for new-product strategy.

duction processes. It possesses the capacity to operate these processes better than anyone else.

The shaded area in Figure 5 represents your current operations. Your new product will lie *outside* that area by definition. How far outside, and in which direction (new markets or new processes) will be determined by your objectives and your company's special strengths. It makes sense to build on your competitive advantage.

Thus, if your long suit is the markets you serve, your next successful new product may lie some distance away from home base along the horizontal axis. If your company's expertise is in a particular technology or is based on unique equipment, your ideal new product will lie along the vertical axis, above the shaded area.

PLAYING THE PERCENTAGES

Once the groundwork is laid and you have established the criteria for the new product, you can set about generating fitting new-product concepts. The next step is to look to the outside world—for trends, changes, discontinuities, different perspectives, ingenious combinations, fresh insights—anything relevant to your new-product criteria.

Remember, however, that the business environment within which your company operates today has become very complex and diverse. Figure 6 depicts the growth of the world's population over the past 10,000 years. I submit that the same Malthusian proliferation applies to technology (and to information generally). There are now more than 100,000 technical journals published throughout the world; 72 billion new pieces of information came into the world last year. One thousand new books are published every day. The total body of information is now doubling every ten years. Indeed, 75 percent of our current knowledge has been developed in the last two decades. The National Science Foundation reports that the technical information received by a chemical engineer in the class of 1960 became essentially obsolete by 1965. Similar rates of obsolescence apply in other technical fields—transportation, communications, medicine.

Under these circumstances, it is clear that any task of significant breadth—such as the conception of potential new products for your company—is a complex undertaking that calls for a vast amount of information and expertise. Thus the solution to the problem is not to seek that single omniscient human being who can come up with the perfect next new product for your company—no such person exists. Instead, play the percentages!

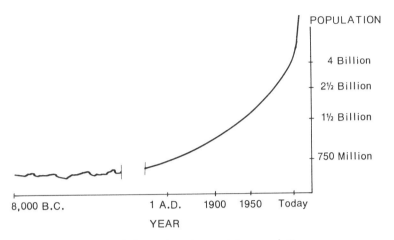

Figure 6. Growth in the world's population.

Draw together a number of forward-looking specialists, each having expertise in a different field that is relevant in some way to potential new products for your company. Then lead them, stimulate them, encourage them, to generate a number of possible candidates for an "acceptable" new product for your company. (Acceptable, in terms of the minimum specifications you establish in the beginning.)

These experts may come from inside or outside your company. Whether they have contributed to the success of current or past products of your company is not germane to the task. It is their ability to contribute to the conception of possible *future* products for your company that's important. Get the right people—wherever they come from.

Once your group of experts has generated all the possibilities it can, feed the "candidate" new-product concepts to a hand-picked team of executives *within* the firm, those who are responsible for the functions that will contribute to future profits. From their intimate knowledge of your company's main strengths, and your goals, they can help you refine and select those new-product concepts with the highest potential for success.

To summarize the key points presented in this chapter:

◇ Any firm, in any industry, needs a flow of new products to survive.

◇ It's not economically feasible to develop (or partially develop) a lot of new products in order to distill the few winners.

◇ The starting point should not be new concepts themselves, but a definition of the attributes of the ideal new product for your company.

◇ A future orientation is essential: yesterday's successes have nothing to do with tomorrow's winners.

◇ In the complex world of today, you've got to play the numbers game—many contributors leading to many possibilities.

◇ Once your best people have refined and selected the new-product candidates passing muster, your company can invest in the development of these new products with a high expectation of success.

5

CORPORATE INNOVATION

Small companies and independent inventors now account for a disproportionately large number of the most important inventions and discoveries in the United States. To put it another way, over the past 20 years large firms have produced fewer innovations per unit of sales volume than have small firms. Small companies, it seems, are just better at new-product development than big companies. (See Table 1.)

This is true, whether you measure "largeness" by total sales of the firm, by total number of employees, by total capital investment, or by mean capital investment per employee. Indeed, I suspect that those very measures of largeness have something to do with lack of innovation. For similar reasons, I suspect that a negative correlation would exist between the age of a firm and the innovativeness it exhibits.

"Sure," you may say, "my established, successful, large firm has a lot to lose, while those fledgling firms have very little to lose, and everything to gain, by taking a flyer. Lots of them go bust and cause nary a ripple! Yet I know some do make it big!"

Table 1. Some important contributions of independent inventors and small organizations in the twentieth century.

INVENTION	INVENTOR	INVENTION	INVENTOR
Xerography	Chester Carlson	Jet engine	Frank Whittle and Hans Von Ohain
DDT	J. R. Geigy & Co.		
Insulin	Frederick Banting	Self-winding wristwatch	John Harwood
Vacuum tube	Lee De Forest	Continuous hot-strip rolling of steel	John B. Tytus
Rockets	Robert Goddard		
Streptomycin	Selman Waksman	Helicopter	Juan De La Cierva, Heinrich Focke, and Igor Sikorsky
Penicillin	Alexander Fleming		
Titanium	W. J. Kroll		
Shell molding	Johannes Croning	Mercury dry cell	Samuel Ruben
		Power steering	Francis Davis
Cyclotron	Ernest O. Lawrence	Kodachrome	L. Mannes and L. Godowsky, Jr.
Cotton picker	John and Mack Rust		
		Air conditioning	Willis Carrier
Shrink-proof knitted wear	Richard Walton	Polaroid camera	Edwin Land
Dacron polyester fiber "Terylene"	J. R. Whinfield and J. T. Dickson	Heterodyne radio	Reginald Fessenden
		Ball-point pen	Ladislao and George Biro
Catalytic cracking of petroleum	Eugene Houdry	Cellophane	Jacques Brandenberger
Zipper	Whitcomb Judson and Gideon Sundback	Tungsten carbide	Karl Schroeter
		Bakelite	Leo Baekeland
		Oxygen steel-making process	C. V. Schwarz and J. Miles
Automatic transmissions	H. F. Hobbs		
Gyrocompass	A. Kaempfe, E. A. Sperry, and S. G. Brown	Frequency modulation radio	Edwin Armstrong

Courtesy of Dr. Basil Bard CBE, London, England.

The answer, for the large firm, cannot be to "stand pat and go with a winner." That's a loser's game in the long run. Just how long is governed by the industry in which your company operates. The technology of your industry is advancing at some average rate; the markets you serve are changing at some average rate. To prove it to yourself, look back five years—how many of your current products weren't even being made then? What proportion of your total revenues in the future is likely to come from products that don't even exist now? In the long run, a company, any company, must innovate or deteriorate.

We must not confuse and commingle two separate and distinct issues. Innovation—generating the spark, spawning the possible breakthrough—is one thing. Evaluating—making the investment decision—is quite another. Evaluating the alternatives is fairly easy, and standard procedures exist in every well-managed company for allocating resources among competing projects. But the first issue—coming up with good new-product concepts—can be very difficult in the typical "established, successful, large firm."

ORGANIZING FOR NEW-PRODUCT DEVELOPMENT

How should a large corporation organize for new-product development? How should that function be integrated into the existing organizational structure? And who actually does it? What kind of guy will succeed in generating new products for your company?

Let's deal first with the question of organization—where the new-product development director (or whatever he's called) reports in.

In the case of corporate growth by acquisition rather than by internal start-up, the business world has solved that problem. Companies know what to call the executive in charge here—he's the "director of corporate development"—and they know where he should report in—to the VP of finance. I suppose that's because the process is essentially evaluative rather than innovative in nature, and it's predominantly numbers-oriented. The great Controller in the Sky sayeth that whenever two or three numbers are gathered together, ratios and percentages shall be made of them. In the case of an acquisition candidate, the historical numbers are there, and so they do get "worked," according to the individual acquiring company's favorite formulas.

The other reason the world is so sure that the director of corporate development should report to the financial VP is that it always takes big money (or near-money) to acquire a new company—and sometimes that's all it takes.

New-product development is primarily an innovative process, and there aren't any historical numbers because nothing exists yet. It is not a finance-oriented activity. New-product development is carried out in the arenas of engineering (can we design it?), production (can we make it?), and marketing (can we sell it?)—and the financial projections come in from those quarters.

For new-product development, it takes a lot of R&D by engineering, a lot of cut-and-try by production, and a lot of market research by marketing. All of which has a cost, to be sure. But that cost is often invisible in the beginning. It is diffused among several departmental budgets early on, and after the new-product concept does attain the status of a "project," the cost of its development is spread out over a period of time in controllable, albeit increasing, increments.

From the standpoint of financial commitment, the acquisition of a company can be likened to jumping off a cliff. It's a binary decision—either you do it or you don't do it. On the other hand, new-product development is more like walking down a hill that grows steadily steeper: you can go part way and abort at any time.

By the time a new-product development project demands sufficiently large incremental investments to warrant critical appraisal by management, the concept should be thoroughly defensible, supported by the results of the work funded by earlier, smaller investments. Otherwise, the project *should* be killed.

If new-product development doesn't follow that pattern, something's fishy. The director of new ventures of a major chemicals company recently noted that he had received a request for $60,000, for the third year in a row, to fund continuing development on a particular project. He decided to turn the request down, because the project was obviously not making headway. If it had been, he pointed out, the funds requested would have been up to about $200,000 by then. The R&D engineer apparently just wanted to continue fishing around in a technology he'd been toying with for a couple of years. He hadn't yet succeeded in bringing a new-product concept out of his laboratory—where it would be followed by the cut-and-try by Production and the market research by Marketing.

DEFINING THE SLOT

Back to the original question. For the new-product concept that *does* come out of the closet, who shepherds it through the corporation, and what department in the organization does that person report to? Where should the responsibility lie?

Let's consider the possibilities. The functional departments providing the major input to the total task are R&D/Engineering, Production, Sales, and Finance—not necessarily in that order; not necessarily in *any* order.

What's the main job of an executive in these respective departments? How is his performance evaluated? Why does he get raises and promotions?

◇ The *R&D scientist* is an investigator. He's paid to get the answers—right answers, exact answers, complete answers. And the longer he works on a given concept, the more aspects he finds to investigate and the more he falls in love with the object of his growing expertise.

Yet when the new-product concept is still incomplete, inexact, and probably wrong, it must be checked out for produceability by Production and for marketability by Marketing. As a matter of fact, the concept itself must be permitted to change to reflect feedback from those two sources. It must also be permitted to die, at this early stage, before any more R&D is put into it.

◇ The *production manager* is a doer. He's paid to produce the maximum quantity in the shortest time—high quality ("yield" or "recovery," meaning low scrap), low cost. The way he does that is to adopt and maintain standard production processes. He locks in what works. Long runs. Minimum variations. Balancing interdependent operations. Keep that line humming! "Management by exception."

Yet the alien new product is disruptive to his smooth operations. It requires short runs, of many variations, in the beginning. It may take a machine out of commission. In the beginning, he's producing nothing *but* scrap, at extraordinary costs. He doesn't know how to make that thing—he's never done it before. On the learning curve, he's *nowhere*. Takes forever to get the first good one! The new product is the "exception"—to be managed, somehow.

◇ The *sales manager* is paid, ultimately, to bring in orders—as large as possible, as many as possible. The total volume of business he brings in during the period is what he's evaluated on. The size of his job—the number of calls he could make, prospects whose business he could solicit—is infinite. He plays the odds and goes after the big ones, the quick hitters. He's *got* to meet his bogey this year, if not this month!

The volume of sales contributed by the new product this year will be negligible. It's hard to learn its new features, functions, and benefits—and the salesman may have to call on new prospects he's never met before. Instead of *selling* anything in the beginning, he probably has to *give* it away, maybe even persuade the first customer to try it once. In any case, this distraction from his main efforts will not be particularly welcome. He may have more important things to do.

◇ The *controller* fulfills his fiduciary responsibility by being the gatekeeper—the conscience of the company. He is paid to husband the firm's resources, play "devil's advocate," be "bottom-line" oriented. Conservatism is his watchword. He doesn't take flyers. Saying yes is a no-win proposition for the financial man.

Yet the new-product concept that ultimately proves to be a winner may be quite unconventional. There may be no precedent on which to rely, and it may be a real gamble. The new-product manager of a pharmaceuticals firm recently told me that he had just run a study which *proved* that it is no longer worthwhile for any company in his industry to develop the "average" new product. It makes sense only to develop the next Valium, that's all! And who's to know in advance?

Make no mistake: none of the above should be construed as the least bit critical of the typical perspectives of executives from these four functional areas. They are doing their respective jobs. You wouldn't have it any other way!

It's just that the goals of these responsible executives are not in harmony with the activities necessary to bring new products on stream. Yet new-product development is, in the long run, the life blood of the company. It is at least as important to the company as a whole as any *one* of the functions relating to ongoing operations. So where does it fit? Who should do the job, and where does that important person report in the organization?

I'll tell you who *shouldn't* do it: the new-product development committee. Why? Because it doesn't work. An executive of a major old-line hardware manufacturer in Los Angeles told me recently that his company had set up a new-product development committee composed of members from each major functional area. They meet regularly to evaluate new-product concepts from any source. He told me that everyone seems to feel a built-in compulsion to kill—loudly and strongly—any new idea proposed. For example, he explained, silence from the financial member of the committee is tantamount to "no objection; go ahead." It is therefore important that any new-product concept be stomped to death in the meeting, so that nobody outside the room could possibly be left with any misapprehension, and actually develop a new product. The approach has been eminently successful: the committee has not approved one new product in five years!

Therefore the only way out, by default, is to assign the job to a new-product development director. That person must report to the general manager of the company or of the division, or operating unit, of the corporation. And he must have equal clout with all the heads of the functional activities related to the division's current operations. Most disputes between functional heads can then be settled by negotiation. Those that can't be are properly referred to the general manager for resolution, based on his balancing of short-run and long-run considerations. That works!

FILLING THE SLOT

Now that we have properly fixed the new-product development slot within the organization, what kind of person should fill that slot? What are the characteristics and abilities of the successful new-product development director? What do we look for in a person who can handle the job?

Young	I've never met an old one.
Bright	He has to come up to speed quickly and thoroughly in alien technologies and markets. Enough to earn him credibility.
Multifaceted	He has to become conversant with all aspects—technical, marketing, financial—of each new-product concept. And he'd better have several going at once.
Persevering	It's not easy. The new-product concept has zero status in the company; its "competitors"—the current production lines—are bringing in the income.
Unflappable	He'll receive a lot of criticism and meet adversity at every turn.

Diplomatic   He's got to rely on goodwill, favors, bootlegging,
               and "government jobs" to get the concept through
               the informal, unfunded, early stages.
Secure   Others will seize the winners and run with them,
               claiming the credit. He'll be left the blame for the
               turkeys.

That's all it takes. Catch your new-product development director
early, though. Some burn out fast. There are lots of easier ways
to make a living. Others run dry or get bored after a while and
seek other fields to romp in.

6

LEADING
FROM
STRENGTH

A cardinal rule I would propose for profitable expansion and extension of a business—any business—is: "Go with what you have going for you." You have earned a position. You have built up an equity (in the broadest sense) by doing whatever it is your company does, for a long time—successfully. You are "there." Now it makes sense to build from that plateau, leveraging the unique position you have attained.

What a manufacturing company *does*—the line functions of operation—is the mainstream of its business. A company makes things and sells things. That's it. All the other functions that are performed in the organization are subsidiary and exist only to support the making and the selling. Designing, purchasing, borrowing money, managing, training, advertising, accounting, testing, planning—and any other functions you can think of that are commonly carried on in a manufacturing organization—serve either the production or the marketing of the product of that firm.

Either one of these line functions may constitute the company's long suit. So when the company begins to think about expanding or extending its core business, it should look first at its current special strengths—in the technical/production area, or in the marketing area. The company may have based its success to date on a technological capacity or unique manufacturing capability (including both machines and "black art"). Or its success may stem primarily from "muscle in the marketplace" (through longstanding relations with distributors, ability to get shelf space from retailers, widespread brand recognition by consumers, or simply "doing it with mirrors").

In either case, *that* should be the company's starting point in conceiving additional new products. Let's consider, in turn, building new business on a technology/capital equipment base and building on a consumer distribution/brand base.

GOING WITH YOUR MAIN MACHINES

Nobody takes exception to the proposition that a company— any company—exists to serve its market. Beyond that, we are admonished not to be nearsighted as to what or who our "market" is. The example often used is that the railroad companies wouldn't be in the state they are in today if they had perceived themselves, half a century ago, as being "not in the railroad business but in the transportation business." Espousing this grand strategy, the argument continues, the railroad companies in the early 1930s should have entered the trucking industry and the airlines industry as well (regulations permitting).

I think not. I'd like to offer some leavening to that philosophy, from a pragmatic viewpoint, defining the "last" to which an individual company should stick—especially in these times. My argument should also assuage the conscience of chief executive officers who have been feeling a little guilty about the lack of grandiosity in their plans.

The argument applies to manufacturing companies, and particularly capital-intensive manufacturing companies. My main assumption—and this immediately gives away the whole point in advance—is that *producing* is capital-intensive; *selling* is not.

Current Versus Future Business

Manufacturing companies, to a greater or lesser extent, have invested heavily in the machinery, materials handling systems, and other supporting capital equipment to produce their *current* products. Before that kind of investment decision is made, there is much planning, analyzing, forecasting, and assessment of future possibilities. Then, finally, it's time for bullet biting— committing the funds, implementing the management decision to go ahead, entering the business.

The same sort of hard decision-making precedes the *expansion* of facilities—adding capacity, upgrading equipment, modernizing the plant. Once you make the decision, and implement it, you're stuck with what you've got. You're committed—locked in—for some future period.

Now the prudent manager will cover his bet (on the future) by providing for some flexibility. If the projected market is 300 K units annually, 8 million tons per year, or whatever, the prudent manager will build in capacity to handle greater than that volume—by some margin. Similarly, he will probably opt for a greater capacity than currently required (for example, a new 120 inch mill, when the largest plate currently sold is 100 inches wide). He will have higher speeds built in, greater combinations possible—just in case things change.

So whether initiating the business or expanding the business, the manufacturer commits, up front, to a capability to produce—for some period in the future. The company has taken its stand.

Some time later (and that's significant) these production facilities will come on stream and be available to produce something. What thing? The particular line of products the company is selling in the marketplace. The company is "there."

And it will be there, for some time to come. Just as a company does not quickly begin producing, so it does not soon cease producing, nor does it readily change the nature of its production operations. You have to feed the baby. Once committed, you're asset-bound! You have to keep the machinery—*that* machinery—working on something. You have to get your bait back!

On the other hand, marketing operations are not that phlegmatic. You can decide to enter a market, and do it, in pretty short order. You can spend the necessary promotional dollars, you can tie in with sales-rep organizations that already have an established reputation in their field; you can hire some marketing/sales people who know their way around in a particular market. A manufacturer can develop a good strategy to penetrate any market, whether or not the company has ever been there.

You can also get out, pretty quickly. The company can summarily abandon a market, new or old, bury the bodies, and walk away. There will be no tangible evidence of the excursion—no in-place reminders of a bad decision, a faulty prediction on the part of management. Older, more specialized employees can be retired, retrained, or fired; younger, more versatile employees can be reassigned and absorbed.

There is nothing to *protect* your marketing strategies, either—except "getting there first," preempting a position in the marketplace. No special patents, no secret process or formula, no unique machinery or "black art" can be relied upon to maintain your position in the market.

The bottom line is: a manufacturing firm is married to the technology and the production facilities and processes it already possesses, at least in the short run. But it is not married to any given market; the company is free to exploit or capitalize on its production capabilities in any market.

The New York, New Haven & Hartford Railroad should not have gone into the airlines business in the 1930s, even if it could have. (However, maybe it *should* have been the one to start the Victoria Station restaurant chain.) American Can Company should not have gone into the glass bottle business, but it did (perceiving itself to be "in the container business"). Things didn't work out. What does American Can know about glass bottles? No hundred-year-old lock company has yet entered the business of manufacturing new, high-security, rotary-disc-cylinder locks. Takes a different kind of equipment and processes than the old pin-tumbler locks. The production process is better suited to mechanical watch companies, which, incidentally, need that kind of product more than they need an electronic watch line (which they don't know a lot about).

For its own good, a company should not get too sophisticated in its management philosophizing. Continuing to engage in the same type of production process will gain you a lot more credibility in the marketplace than making a management decision to change gears—a decision that may be viewed as hedging your bet on the market you have served for years, in anticipation of the day when the underlying technology moves on.

Unless it works for you, there's no point stubbornly defending your share of a given market. That doesn't get you extra points, necessarily. The point is to keep doing what you're best at. If a new technology comes along that effectively supplants your product—your "approach to filling the customer's need"—don't feel constrained by the binary choice of fighting the competition or joining them. You don't *have* to resist the inevitable. Nor do you have to try to do something you've never done before and something your capital equipment is not suited to. There's another option: you can walk away from it. You can concentrate on a more profitable objective—namely, figuring out how best to redeploy your fixed assets into more productive uses.

The record shows that, by and large, the major breakthroughs in any industry (read, "market served") have come from sources or companies *outside* that industry. Don't fight it. And don't feel compelled to hop on the bandwagon (late) of those who are eroding your market. You don't have to do that either. There are other options available, other markets, perhaps new needs, that your company and its production facilities can satisfy.

In the literature of corporate planning, analyses are frequently made of the "strengths and weaknesses" of a given company. It should be made clear that concern for "weaknesses" applies only to maintaining the *current* business and has nothing to do with future growth into new fields. It's essentially a defensive posture. Similarly, in the case of analyses of the "threats and opportunities" that a given company faces, the "threats" relate only to the possible diminishment of market share, or total sales, of *current* products.

For solid corporate growth, it is necessary to adopt a positive stance, exploiting the company's strengths and capitalizing on relevant opportunities available. A firm's strengths should serve, in part at least, to *determine* its goals, rather than being looked upon merely as the means to achieving those goals.

Building on Assets

If you accept this proposition, the question then becomes: What can your company produce with its current facilities and equipment, besides more of the same—additional models and variations (product-line extensions) and natural by-products of the process? The answer may be, "Quite a number of other products!" Your current product line is just one avenue by which you have chosen to exhibit the capabilities of your production equipment and the technologies in which you have competence. There are other avenues, almost certainly!

There may not be a whole lot of other things you can produce with *all* your machines and equipment—in exactly the same condition and in the same sequence of processes you are now using. As they now stand, they in effect *define* your present end product. But to the extent that your capital equipment is not dedicated (to the manufacture of one product) and to the extent that the various operations are, or can be utilized as, batch processes rather than continuous, interdependent, in-line processing—to that extent your facilities can be adapted to the manufacture of other products.

New dies, new molds, new jigs and fixtures, a different order of operations—maybe a new raw material. But use the capital equipment you've got. That's your main, leverageable asset. You have to keep your main machines working—those that you (especially) know how to work.

Which are your "main machines," the assets you are most interested in keeping productive? That's simply a function of three attributes of any piece of capital equipment: (1) How big an investment does it represent? (2) How new is it? (3) How unique is it? That's where the payoff is.

But my main point is that *equipment* is the key to future growth. Your firm's management should not look at one of its plants, the product of which is outmoded or suddenly facing grim prospects for future revenue, and ask, "What can we produce in that plant?" Rather, management should ask: (1) What equipment in that plant is it most important to keep in action? (2) How must the equipment be modified to do a new job? (3) What additional capital equipment should be purchased to combine with and support that equipment?

It is essential to do a thorough job of market research before committing yourself to production of the new product. It is possible that, impelled by the strong desire to utilize certain equipment, you'll end up manufacturing something you love to produce but nobody wants to buy! In other (and more) words, you have to ascertain, as best you can, that there will be sufficient volume of sales at a price level adequate to cover your variable costs and make at least a significant contribution to the fixed burden of the capital equipment.

For starters, you have to recognize that you will be serving new customers and facing different competitors, and the game may be played quite differently than it was with your former product.

The new product will possess its own special attributes. Care must be taken not to adopt too simplistic an approach to the marketplace. You can't go to "the" market with a story on the features, functions, and benefits of this new material, or chemical, or gadget, or system. There probably will be a number of different markets for the new product or variations of it. Certain features or functions may offer great benefits in one market and be totally irrelevant in other markets.

For example, a new composite material may be valued for its high strength-to-weight ratio in one application and for its high lubricity in another. The inherent corrosion resistance of a new high-security lock may be very important to cruise ship operators, but totally irrelevant to hotel owners, for whom ease in changing the combination is paramount.

The market researcher should "go fishing" in several markets and be sensitive to feedback on the perceived value of any of the attributes of the proposed new product in its various applications. It is likely that different volumes of sales, different prices, and different promotion and distribution policies will be applicable to the (essentially identical) product when it is sold in different markets for different purposes. The capital equipment you use to manufacture it won't know the difference—and that way you can keep your "main machines" humming.

GOING WITH YOUR BRAND

There are more than 300,000 brand names floating around out there. Among them, there are good brands, bad brands, and irrelevant brands. For the international firm, this is true in *spades!* The French word for "spades" (the strongest and winning suit) is *pique.* Vachon, Inc., a manufacturer located just outside Quebec City, enjoys a very profitable business from the distribution of its snack product "Pique" within the largely French-speaking province of Quebec. In order to further its expansion and growth, Vachon made a management decision to introduce this high-volume, profitable product in the neighboring province of Ontario. For that market, it was felt that an English brand name would be more suitable than a French one; so the ad agency, in its wisdom, translated the name directly. Vachon introduced "Spades" in Ontario. It bombed. The company has withdrawn the product from that market. It was a bad brand.

There is a pencil manufacturer in this country (whose identity, for me at least, is not unforgettable) that introduced a brand of lead pencil called "Caron d'Ache." Those of you who speak French will pronounce it correctly (without phonetic assistance, such as supplied by Nestlé); and those of you who understand Russian will recognize that the word

КАРАНДШ

means "pencil." But how big a market segment do those people who speak French and understand Russian comprise in America? So why bother? Berol, Inc., a pencil manufacturer in Danbury, Connecticut, will tell you that there is not a lot of strong brand loyalty in this highly competitive market, anyway—not even among us literate folks who use lead pencils. The selection and use of a particular brand may make the seller feel better, but "nobody knows you did it," as the saying goes. It's irrelevant.

What Makes a Brand Name Good?

There are good brands. The company I referred to earlier, Vachon, Inc., recently changed its name and family brand to "Culinar." That will probably be a good brand name, for all the classic reasons. The company itself has high confidence in it, as evidenced by this statement in its annual report:

> For the consumer, the symbol will stand as a seal of quality which inspires confidence.
>
> Culinar, Inc. is also a name easily adapted to all our *expansion and diversification needs.* (Emphasis mine.)

What makes a brand name "good" in the beginning? The bottom line is: it's a good brand if it helps you introduce a new product, if it induces the consumer—enough consumers—to give it a shot. In the beginning, it's important to select (or fabricate) a brand name that will do just that. Whatever name you use must strike some chord with consumers, arising from their "experience-based perspective," that causes them to buy your new product for the first time.

Later, after consumers have tried and liked your product, and after your have aggressively promoted your brand name, that favorable association between your product and your brand will become a *part* of consumers' "experience-based perspective." In the case of a food product, you are what they eat—and you will have established a "consumer franchise" (in the jargon of the trade) for your brand. Consumers will try once almost any new product you elect to cloak with that mantle.

But in order to retain and enhance your "franchise," you must take great care to ensure that consumers *consistently* have good experience with products bearing your brand. That will make the brand stronger. It is a symbiotic relationship: the brand helps the products, and the products help the brand. That's obvious, and most of the literature on the subject deals with whether or not to attach an established "family brand" (as multiple-product brands are called) to a given new product. And most management decisions in this area are directed to the question: "Diet Pepsi" or "Tab"?

Products for Brands, Not Brands for Products

But I would like to go back two squares. Where does this "given new product" come from? Who "gives" it to management, so that binary whether-or-not branding decision can be made? Is it the R&D lab? Your field salesforce? "Market research"? The production department? Are you knocking off a competitor's product? Wherever they come from, these "given new products" generally exhibit one or more of these characteristics:

1. They are usually pretty "close to home"—a minor variation or product-line extension.
2. They probably will not succeed—in at least nine out of ten cases, they don't.
3. They will cost you a lot of money by the time you get to the test market—and they still may fail.

That's what the record shows. Therefore, accepting the "gift"—the given new product—from the conventional sources for the binary branding decision just may not be the best way to go. In point of fact, that may be just the reverse of the sequence of activities appropriate to ensuring sound corporate growth. Perhaps the brand itself—rather than the new-product idea—is the best place to start.

In other words, you can get there by generating new-product ideas that fit your brand to start with, rather than deciding whether to fit your brand to a "given new product." The brand is a major element in the construction of the target. The brand itself can be instrumental in generating the good new products; it should not serve only as an "award" to, and a vehicle for selling, "given new products." So use the brand itself as a point of departure, along with other "assets," or peculiar strengths, that can be exploited to give your company an edge—the special advantage that will enable you to introduce a new product successfully and sustain its profitability in the marketplace.

With respect to the brand name, "exploit" is the wrong word. That implies that you are drawing from, or somehow depleting, an asset. A brand is more like a muscle—the more you use it properly, the stronger it gets. The brand gives you *leverage* in the market.

Your brand is unique to you. It possesses demonstrable value to your company. A good brand is, by definition, an under-exploited—a less than maximally leveraged—asset. It has potential that you are not utilizing, so you are *never* gaining the full return on your investment in that asset.

Your company may well have other unique, underutilized assets that can help you further corporate growth through the successful introduction of new products. Excess gun-drilling capacity, fiber-optics technology, low-cost electric power, specialized management ability, an exclusive license—all such assets should constitute the first leg of your new-product tripod—the base from which you build new products to foster corporate growth.

The second leg consists of your objectives and goals, especially involving matters of finance, timing, and competitive position.

The third leg of the base from which you expand your business includes all the constraints within which your company operates—the policies and prejudices that, together, make up your corporate style.

Again, the place to start in planning for corporate growth, whether by acquisition or by new-product development, is with *your company's style, objectives, and unique assets*—and one of those assets is your brand, which (if a good one) can never be fully leveraged. That's square 1: your "success criteria." They will spell out the characteristics of the ideal new product for your company.

PART TWO

THE
STRATEGIC
INNOVATION
PROCESS

7

STRATEGIC
INNOVATION
AND NEW-PRODUCT
DEVELOPMENT

"My organization is engaged in the _____ business." Let's analyze that simple statement.

First of all, why do you need an "organization"? Why must an organization be formed to do what you are now doing? Think about it! There are only two reasons I can think of.

1. The job's too big. You yourself simply cannot *physically* do all that needs to be done. You've got to recruit some additional hands to help out.

2. The job's too complex. You simply cannot *mentally* do all the parts of the job. Nobody can be a specialist in that many areas. So you go out and get, not simply more hands, but different hands.

From there, everything else follows—the planning, the assignment of responsibilities, the delegation of authority, the direction and control. And you "engage in your business."

That's easy. Or at least it's comparatively easy to "engage in"

your own business, from day to day, once you get it going. And when it begins to hum along, that will carry you—for a while. But if there's anything to the product-life-cycle curve (and there is), a while is not forever! You've got to start thinking about the next new product line you will introduce—the next *business* you will engage in—and organize for it.

The basic question is: "What can your company do?"

The answer is: "A lot of things! We can do more of the same—and very well, thank you. We can design and manufacture—and sell, by the way—product-line extensions and refinements and new models of our present products, and we could probably do some other things too."

You surely *can*. Your company could make and sell a *number* of new products that utilize the particular capital equipment and skills you have built up, and that capitalize on the reputation in the marketplace you have earned. But who knows what those perfect new products are—those products that are sure to be successful in today's marketplace? Who can come up with the answers?

"NONSOURCES" OF NEW PRODUCTS

I'd like to suggest three unlikely sources. First, I don't believe that the people within your organization can do it, at least not alone. Remember, you have recruited and hired specialists to help you carry on the business that your organization is *currently* engaged in. So most of those on your payroll now are pulling their weight by contributing to your present day-to-day business—and the profits that are derived from it. They also happen to be the world's greatest experts on everything you have done in the past. It would be pure coincidence if any employee just happened to be expert in the ideal new business for your company in the future.

The other main impediment to the conception of a profitable new product by your own people is the plain fact that most of

them are very busy. They are connected in some way to your present, ongoing business—the products that have status, the ones that generate profits—where mistakes and failures are visible.

Are there deadlines in your business? Do you ever have to come through "on time"? Or do you just cruise along doing what you feel like any time? Well, if you ever experience the "eleventh-hour crunch," I think a legitimate question is: Which would take precedence—something that your customer (or your boss, if you've got one) demands by "c.o.b. Tuesday," or something that may pay off three or four years from now? It's not hard to call that shot.

I think there may be a bit of Parkinson's Law operating here as well. People let the various short-term tasks assigned them fill all their time. After all, isn't it easier and more satisfying to achieve a lot of "small" goals—short steps on an approved path—rather than to strike out and try something that nobody has heard of? So I don't think the long-range project will ever get tackled as long as there are enough short-range sure shots in the in-box—and there always will be!

In brief, it's tough to come up with successful new products for your company from *within* the organization. Then where, *outside* your organization, should you look for your ideal next new product?

I'll tell you where not to look. Don't go to a run-of-the-mill management consulting firm. That's the second unlikely source of good new-product ideas for your company. Consultants know only what they know (as a result of past projects). It's too early to opt for an expert in a specific category, unless you are already positive where it is you want to go. It's hard to find a specialist in "everything else"—that is, anything *but* what you are now producing. These days, you cannot find the compleat generalist who knows something about everything. The world has simply become too complex.

The third "nonsource" of good new-product concepts is the

computer. Computers help process and manage the flood of information now upon us, but data banks are a lousy place to look for new-product ideas that are right for your company. It's hard to think of the right question to ask—the key words that will call up new-product concepts suitable to your unique organization. If you had the question, you'd have the answer. Besides, whatever is in the computer is "old hat"—everybody else (including your competitors) has already gone through it. Finally, everything you retrieve from the data bank looks as important as everything else. Somebody has to distinguish the valuable breakthroughs from the nits—to translate objective data into significant meaning for your particular organization.

A SYSTEM THAT WORKS

So how *can* you generate new products for your company that are sure to be successful in the marketplace? The answer is: the Strategic Innovation™ System. I'll outline the steps in the process in sequence below. The system will be explained in greater detail in the following chapters.

Establishing the Criteria for Success

First, you'll want to select from within your organization the executives who represent the different functional areas of your business. They have different perspectives. You have to assemble these people into a team—the project team for this particular task. In each case you need the chief responsible for that particular area—marketing, production, R&D, finance, general management, and "other." What "other" is depends on the nature of your project. Make sure all views are represented, though. You need those from the organization who can and will contribute their specialized knowledge from their area; you need those who

™ A registered trademark of Strategic Innovations, Inc.

have the responsibility and who can and will make judgments for the organization. Finally (defensively), you need to include anyone who could scuttle the effort or veto the results.

That's the project team you'll be working with throughout the program. They lend special expertise—guidance and direction, continuity and coherence—to the effort. Now, let's look at your position. As the person responsible for bringing a successful new product on stream, you have to remain at arm's length from the team. You are not part of the team, but rather serve in the complementary role, providing the cosine, the Yang. Also, you are the catalyst: you make it happen. I suggest you get yourself a buddy—it's definitely a two-man job. You might want to retain a consultant to perform the leader's role. It's more difficult to lead the team when you are stuck within the pecking order of the organization.

At any rate, the leader will conduct the Orientation Briefing—an all-day meeting with the project team to explore the organization's objectives with respect to new products, to determine what the organization "brings to the party" to attain those objectives, and to review any pertinent historical information on successes and failures and any prejudices that may exist regarding future activities. Be sure to tape-record the proceedings and make sure everyone has a say.

Next, review the tapes and make notes. Listen for how early something gets brought out, how many times it's repeated, who says it, how loud it's shouted. That will give you an indication of the relative importance of specific objectives. Draft the criteria that best delineate the ideal new product in terms of the organization's objectives, expressed preferences, and main strengths. A proposed rank, or designation of relative importance, should be attached to each criterion. Three or four levels in a hierarchy are sufficient. It doesn't do to split hairs. Use something like "mandatory," "desired," and "bonus."

Next, the leader should meet with the project team again to

review and affirm—or modify, reorder, eliminate, and add to—any of the proposed criteria for success. They, then, become the charter of the project. Everyone has "signed off."

Developing a Strategy

The next step in the Strategic Innovation Process is the development of a strategy, or the identification of a broad area of opportunity for growth, based on trends that are relevant to your new-product criteria. The criteria established the *what;* the next step establishes the *how to.* It gives you a handle on the task. If you concentrate creative effort within a field of high promise, you simply *have* to come up with a higher proportion of winners than you otherwise would.

At this point you turn your attention away from the "inside." You have passed that stage, and you have a blue-ribbon team representing the organization working *with* you toward the same end. You can now focus on the problem itself, and the attributes of the perfect solution that the criteria set forth.

It's time to look at the outside world within which your organization will introduce this new product in the future. What changes are occurring that are relevant to your criteria? What trends and discontinuities and new relationships can you discern that are pertinent to the task? Are there any critical technological, economic, or regulatory changes? Changes in markets, lifestyles? Remember, timing is everything. You have to sense when the time has come for new ideas that your organization is capable of turning into successful new products. Survey the field for opportunities germane to your firm's criteria.

The Innovation Session

Now, the crucial step: draw together six outside experts, each specializing in a different area and each offering a perspective different from that of anyone on the organization's payroll. (No sense duplicating or second-guessing the expertise you've already got on your team.) The theory is that there are ideas and insights in the *outside* world that will be useful to your organization in forging new businesses or developing new products. (Eventually, you may want to develop a Brain Bank™ of experts in a broad range of fields to call upon as the elements of a given project warrant.) Use consultants, professors, authors, editors, researchers, government professionals, butchers, bakers, doctors, bankers, merchant chiefs—anyone whose expertise is, in your judgment, relevant to some aspect of the task. You must make sure, though, that they are top caliber. They should possess a sufficiently broad perspective and be sufficiently articulate to participate effectively in an Innovation Session.

Prepare these six outside experts in advance by sending them a Briefing Document describing just what you want them to know about the task—to encourage them to do their homework ahead of time. (More about that in Chapter 11.)

After the experts have been duly briefed and prepared, bring them together in the site you have chosen for the Innovation Session. The facility should be off premises and should be prepared specifically for your purpose. For one thing, the meeting room should be "wired." You need to tape-record the Innovation Session so that you don't miss anything.

Members of the project team should not participate in the Innovation Session. They would only inhibit the other participants, and there is great risk that their presence would turn the session into a question-and-answer period and that the leader would lose control. Their turn will come.

Innovation Cycle 1

Conduct the session utilizing standard creative techniques as necessary to stimulate participation, insights, and synergy. Your job is to manage group dynamics, maintaining "pace" and driving the contributors in directions that you feel will be fruitful. The objective is not to "get the right answer," but to generate the

™ Registered trademark of Strategic Innovations, Inc.

maximum number of possibilities. An Innovation Session is a lot like brainstorming. You should observe all the "rules" of brainstorming, especially the rule proscribing negativism or criticism. But there arc a number of differences too, as we will see in Chapter 10.

Following the Innovation Session, review the tapes and combine the individual concepts (whenever they emerged) into logical groupings. Obtain sufficient supplementary data to flesh out any obscure or incomplete ideas. Now you're ready to meet again with the project team. You have obtained the best ideas that the outside world has to offer, and it's time to get the contributions of the best of those inside the organization. With enough quantity to play with, if you do things right, you can't miss.

There's no possibility of preparing the inside team by providing controlled information—they know the whole problem. But what you *can* do now is stimulate their thinking in new directions by presenting them with the fresh ideas from your top-caliber outside experts, people who live in different worlds than any of them have ever lived in.

Explain to the members of the project team that the rules of brainstorming must be observed—no negativism. The purpose of the meeting is not to judge and criticize, but rather to build on the ideas from outside sources. Then feed the "possibilities" in, one at a time, in the sequence you've planned, and encourage the project team to "chew" on them, make them better, and come up with related suggestions and ideas. Your team members are, after all, the experts on what the organization can and will do.

Following that meeting—I call it a Building Session—you conduct the Evaluation Meeting. The benchmarks against which the concepts should be evaluated by the project team are the criteria for success agreed to at the outset. (It's hard to hit a moving target, and it's hazardous to get caught in the crossfire.) The question to be answered for each concept is: "Does it measure up? Can it meet at least the most important criteria?"

You can expect some differences of opinion among members

of the project team, because although they are all using the same benchmarks, they each have a different type of knowledge and a different perspective. The important thing is to enable each "judge" to form an opinion initially, without being influenced by the positions of other members of the project team. Then it is your responsibility to lead the "negotiations" on concepts that are in the running. Out of this evaluation process will come some survivors. There always are some concepts that everyone agrees, finally, do hold promise for fulfilling the criteria.

Innovation Cycle 2

What makes the Strategic Innovation System especially productive is the second Innovation Cycle, which keys on the results of the first. You've made progress. You now have the advantage of feedback from members of the project team as to their position on *specific* concepts. You know how they react to actual new-product possibilities.

Armed with that knowledge, you then conduct a follow-up Innovation Session. Assemble six *new* outside experts, this time with greater depth of expertise in narrower fields. Prepare a new Briefing Document, describing the area of concentrated interest and containing some of the winning concepts as seed ideas. You can then conduct a freewheeling, but more focused Innovation Session.

After debriefing the results, again hold a Building Session and an Evaluation Meeting with the project team. This time you will find that you end up with more winners—because you went where they wanted you to go and got more concepts like the ones they liked the first time around.

Qualification

Out of the innovation phase of the project will flow some tentative new-product candidates. And they have a certain amount of stature, because of their source. But so far everybody has been shooting from the hip—purposely, to prevent the premature investment in engineering development and market research on some concept that, ultimately, will never fly. It is now time to check out these new-product concepts.

No new product I know of ever came to market in exactly the same form in which it was originally conceived. So the job before you at this point is to incorporate the changes necessary to render certain concepts viable, support certain concepts in their basic form (refinements to come later), and kill those concepts that will not make it, for one reason or another.

To do that, you must pursue two fundamental areas of investigation for each surviving concept: (1) Can such a product be manufactured by your organization? (2) Can such a product be successfully marketed by your organization? No reason not to undertake these two investigations—the produceability question and the market research work—simultaneously.

You are going to lose some concepts in the process. But that's all right, because you started out with more new-product concepts than your organization could do anything about—at one time, anyway. Those that make the cut, you can have confidence will warrant the investment to develop and launch.

Management Action Plan

Nothing will actually happen unless you take the last step. You've got to get management—the key member(s) of the project team—to select one of the new-product candidates to go with, *now*. Once that decision is made, you have to develop the plan of implementation. Determine all the actions, *in sequence*, that need to be taken—and by whom, and by when—in order to move the new product from the conceptual stage through to successful production and introduction to the market.

That's the entire Strategic Innovation Process. The result is not one but a *number* of specific new-product candidates that exploit your organization's main strengths, respond to identified market opportunities, and have the potential to meet your financial goals. In addition, as an integral part of the process, you will have a tactical plan to implement one new-product introduction.

The process works.

8

ESTABLISHING
SUCCESS
CRITERIA

As noted in the preceding chapter, the first step in the Strategic Innovation Process—establishing success criteria for your firm—is the basis for all your efforts in developing new products.

Few would argue against the desirability of deciding what it is you want to do before you do it. For an organization—a manufacturing company, for example—this means establishing objectives before taking action, objectives for the company as a whole as well as for individual departments or functional divisions.

But much "objective setting," as currently practiced, is past-oriented, defensive, constrictive, and wrong-headed. The objectives that result retard and constrain progress more than they stimulate growth. They are, generally, almost useless for the purpose for which they are designed.

THE FIRM'S CURRENT BUSINESS

Former Harvard professor Harry Levinson, in his book *Organizational Dynamics*, proposed that executives take an introspective look at their company's history in order to make sound management decisions.

A number of consulting firms specialize in profiling a company's "strengths and weaknesses"; some even put different product lines in separate categories in a matrix, and give each a designation, based on their respective profitability and growth potential.

Accurately delineating the characteristics of a firm—its strengths and weaknesses—amounts to a "balance sheet" assessment of where the company *currently* stands as a result of all that has gone before. From there, it is, of course, possible to generalize—to abstract "what business we are really in."

Such preoccupation by management with the company's own navel—in an effort to discern some "grand design"—is practically useless for determining the direction of the firm's future growth. At worst, it culminates in an interesting summary of where the firm *has been*. At best, the abstraction will sufficiently broaden the perspective of management to permit only those additional activities in the future that are very closely related to what the company has done in the past.

That attitude is defensive, unnecessarily limiting, and anachronistic. It requires that each proposed new business activity or product line pass the test of being very close to home—in harmony with past activities—regardless of other considerations.

If management does look up from the company navel to survey the *outside* environment, even the *future* environment, within which the firm will operate, its attention is often focused on "opportunities and threats." That is, opportunities for, and threats to, the maintenance of the firm's vested, narrowly defined, current business.

As noted earlier, "threats" have to do with management caretaking of the current business; they have nothing to do with initiation of new business, development of new products, penetration of new markets, or adoption of new marketing strategies.

That is not to say that the maintenance and security of the

current business of the company is not important. Quite the contrary—that is management's first obligation. Without that, there is no future, there are no new products. It is just that there should be no confusion about when management is engaged in the maintenance/caretaking function and when it is pursuing future new business possibilities.

The president of our auditing firm, an independent CPA, suggested to me recently that our company is in the same business as General Motors and the grocery store down the block— *the business of making money.* I smartly disagreed. We are each pursuing our separate, distinctive businesses, and the money we make is simply the measure, the gauge, of our respective success in doing what we have chosen to do.

In the establishment of your future objectives, the financial targets and growth rates are essential as benchmarks to enable you to tell, after the fact, whether you have achieved your goals or not. But they, in themselves, won't help you to get there.

THE FIRM'S FUTURE DIRECTION

What are "objectives" good for, anyway? What are you going to do with them? Just monitor results? Can't they also serve as *positive guides* to help you expand the growth of your company? Yes, they can! Properly framed objectives can actually assist you in accomplishing what you're trying to do.

At the outset of any program to generate new business opportunities for your company, you will want to explore three general areas:

1. *Goals.* What is it that the company absolutely requires? What are its minimum goals?
2. *Assets.* What is it you bring to the table? What are your unique strengths, the "assets" that can be brought to the task of achieving your goals?
3. *Style.* What are the parameters within which the goals must be met? What's the company's style?

You're seeking out your company's minimum demands for the future—its special capabilities and its ground rules.

A brief aside: It's Harry Levinson's theory that no company can properly set goals without a "sense of its own history." I must take exception to this view. I don't believe a company must necessarily be bound by its past. I believe the ground rules for the future can be *expressly stipulated* by the current management of the company. Things change.

Under the heading "Goals," you'll want to consider:
Minimum revenue (by when?)
Minimum profit (ditto)
Market share
Maximum development time
Other goals

Under the heading "Assets," you should include:
Technical knowledge
In-place capital equipment
Manufacturing know-how
Marketing muscle
Available financial resources
Marketplace position
Other special capabilities

Under the heading "Style," you should take into account:
Preferred route to protection from competition
Geographical considerations
Allowable departures from current activities
Relationship with other divisions
Pricing
Production runs
Complexity of technology
Means of implementation (start-up, acquisition, or both)
Image (public and corporate)
Prejudices
Other "ways" of operating

THE SOURCE OF SUCCESS CRITERIA

Where do statements of success criteria come from? Who represents "management"? Who is knowledgeable in all these areas? The answer is: no one. It is impossible for any one person to be totally competent in all facets of the business. Furthermore, no single person has the authority to make decisions in all areas. These are, essentially, the two premises of organization—that's *why* and *how* organizations organize.

Therefore, the team that generates the company's objectives, or success criteria, must be made up of a number of responsible executives. At least five functional areas must be represented:

Technology	(director of R&D?)
Marketing	(vice president of sales?)
Manufacturing	(vice president of production?)
Finance	(controller?)
General management	(president?)

Each person is there to represent his functional perspective and must have the authority to speak for his department.

There are other important considerations in selecting the members of the team:

◇ Members should all be compatible. You don't need the distraction of jousting and sniping.

◇ They should be respected and capable of making things happen. Nominal titleholders and lame ducks don't have the necessary impact.

◇ They should be friendly, open, positive, and "loose." They must be alert to creative ideas, welcoming and encouraging new possibilities.

◇ They should be assertive and verbal, actively participating in and contributing to the work of the group.

◇ The person who ultimately will implement the new business venture, product line, or marketing strategy should be included in the group. The "champion" should be there, to help form the new idea in the beginning—to be a part of it, and it a part of him.

DEVELOPING CRITERIA

The management team should meet for the better part of a day, to provide the input from which the success criteria eventually will be drafted. This initial all-day meeting—the Orientation Briefing—should be tape-recorded. It should be led by two or more people who are not stuck somewhere within the pecking order of the organization. Ideally, they should be perceptive outsiders. The leaders must set the tone. They should inquire naively, probe, press, challenge—and resolve inconsistencies. They must not intimidate or be intimidated. They must ferret out the visceral (gut) reactions as well as the rational (intellectual) responses, both of which ultimately determine what new direction the company can and will take and how far afield it has the courage to venture.

Following the Orientation Briefing, over the next week or so, you as the leader should review the tape recording of the meeting and draft the proposed success criteria. These are a series of point-by-point statements that, taken together, define the *attributes* of the ideal solution, from the company's point of view, tempered by what, in your view, is realistically attainable. And these separate, distinct, proposed criteria should be ranked in order of relative importance.

In formulating the proposed criteria, you will want to "test" each one.

◇ Is it practical and attainable? Never mind what they said—is it *real*? Can a minimum requirement be reduced? Could a maximum investment be raised, under ideal conditions? Could the time period for achievement be extended?

◇ Has the criterion been expressed positively? Trying to eliminate everything that should be ruled out is a never-ending task fit for Sisyphus. You'll help yourself by delineating the characteristics of a *winner*.

◇ Is it "clean and simple"? Does it deal clearly with one feature, or at most a combination of attributes that naturally belong together?

◇ Does each criterion jibe with the other criteria for success? Is everything in line, everything stated on the same basis?

◇ Is the criterion necessary? Will it actually help you do the job? Alternately, will it help in evaluating the possibilities you do come up with?

◇ What is the relative importance of the criterion in the view of the top shooters in the company?

Finally, look them all over—those attributes of the perfect solution. Did you forget anything? Has something been left out? Have you failed to deal with a crucial characteristic whose omission may forever haunt the effort? Make sure you get all key aspects out in the open, up front.

THE REVIEW

Once you have drafted the proposed success criteria and then estimated their relative importance, you need to submit them to the (same) management team for review and confirmation—or modification and confirmation. Each member of the team will, in effect, be "signing off," or agreeing in advance that any concept that appears to meet these success criteria will warrant approval.

When reviewing the proposed criteria with the management team, you must make clear that they are intended not as a profile of the firm's *current* business, but rather as a description of the characteristics of the ideal *next* new business for the company. This constitutes the first cut—narrowing down the field of possibilities to manageable size. That's helpful in doing the job. It will aid you in focusing the efforts to conceive viable new products. And you will therefore get more hits than misses.

You will find unanimity among members of the management team on some of the success criteria, and differences of opinion and disparate judgments on other criteria. That's to be expected. The purpose of reviewing the criteria with team members is to develop consensus. It is my experience that policies are often made on the spot, then and there. And sometimes the position of management is formed and settled, with respect to certain issues, by the senior executive present. That's also useful in giving cohesive direction to the organization. The criteria review is an excellent tool for communicating and coordinating the views of managers with different responsibilities in the organization.

Examples of success criteria actually formulated by this process are shown on the following pages.

PUTTING IT TOGETHER

To summarize, objectives for corporate growth should be:

Future-oriented
Positive
Substantive—multifaceted
Specific
Short, plain, and punchy
Helpful in and of themselves
Ranked in order of relative importance

Such objectives can best be established by the key contributors, working in the same room at the same time and led by two or more disinterested parties. The criteria should be set in two stages—exploratory and confirmatory. Team members meet initially to explore possibilities and, later, to reach consensus on the criteria proposed.

At this point, you have constructed a solid target for the direction of creative efforts—complete from the bull's-eye to the outer rings. You know exactly what you aim to achieve.

SUCCESS CRITERIA—CONFIRMED

Growth strategies for _____ Corporation, consisting of new markets, marketing tactics, products, or businesses which:

M   Utilize, at least in part, the company's engineering art and empirical data base.

M   Are in consonance with the company's "functional orientation."

M   Serve markets that can support manufacture and sales of multiple custom-engineered systems.

M   Can achieve a minimum aftertax ROI of _____% and ROS of _____%.

M   Can produce sales not later than mid-19_____.

M   Require less than $_____ total investment the first year for engineering and market development, not to exceed $_____ million aggregate exposure over the entire development period.

D+ Counter threats posed to _____ existing business (for example, by shortages, as perceived by the marketplace, and the introduction of the _____ technology).

D+ Lead to follow-on sales, by _____, of supplies, parts, spares, and so on.

D   Serve markets of minimum total size of $_____ million per year and growing at _____% per year.

D   Result in automatic feedback of market intelligence.

D   Utilize the company's capabilities in engineering documentation.

D   Can achieve a minimum _____% market share in _____ years after introduction.

D   Provide a vehicle for "synergistic cooperation" with others.

B   Require, solely, the abilities of existing and contemplated staff.

B   May increase the company's visibility and prestige in the international marketplace.

KEY

M = MANDATORY   D = DESIRABLE   B = BONUS

SUCCESS CRITERIA—CONFIRMED

New, long-run, nationwide business opportunities (products or services) for _____ Company, implemented by internal initiation or by acquisition:

M   Contributing at least $_____ additional revenue in the first year of commercial operation.

M   With a strong growth rate and possessing a market potential of at least $_____ million annually.

M   Yielding a minimum of $_____ return on investment before taxes.

M— Undertaken not later than _____, 19_____.

M— Requiring not more than $_____ million cash for implementation.

M— Resulting in a majority ownership position for the company.

M— Constituting a "_____ Product" specialty.

D+ Affording some pride of expertise.

D+ Contributing at least $_____ million additional revenue in the first year of commercial operation.

D+ Lending itself to "annuity" sales.

D+ Aimed at a market that includes, or could include, the _____.

D+ Possessing a market potential of at least $_____ million annual sales within five years.

D   Enabling the company to adopt common procedures in filling diverse orders.

D   Leveraging and enhancing the company's reputation for objectivity, integrity, and authoritativeness.

D   Within an industry characterized by concentrated market shares.

D   Providing a niche not susceptible to severe competition.

D— Instrumental in attracting creative management.

B+ _____-oriented.

B+ Proximate for management efficiency—that is, located anywhere between same building/block and two hours' commute.

B   Offering the company an opportunity to augment its present business base (facilities and personnel).

SUCCESS CRITERIA—CONFIRMED

New strategies for _____ Company, consisting of procedures, techniques, programs, changes, additions, and research with respect to the _____ Marketing Systems, which:

M   Result in a "marked" improvement in renewal rate by *new clients* (first and second renewals), "saving" at least _____ clients per year, and resulting in a reduction of at least _____% from current mortality rate.

M   Can be implemented so as to affect renewals in the sales cycle ending September 1, 19_____ (starting October 1, 19_____).

M   Have a permanently favorable effect on renewal rate.

M   Do not adversely affect client service level or new business generation.

D+ Take advantage of and maintain the company's reputation for dignity, essentiality, authority, and concern for the best interests of others, among both sellers and buyers.

D   Require solely the efforts of company personnel, both in the field and at headquarters, for implementation.

D   Do not generate hostile feelings toward the company from any quarter.

D   Result in a higher level of sales revenues in addition to those accounted for by increased renewals.

D   Improve efficiency of the company's salespeople in the field—both in their own view and in terms of actual results.

D   Provide a better understanding of, and new insights into, the decision-making processes regarding renewal.

D   Shed light on "results" question.

D   Make the company a more important factor in the view of client companies' decision makers and take company services out of the category of "advertising" in the view of clients and prospects.

B   Require only policy changes by the company.

B   As a by-product, generate new "models," line extensions, and other businesses.

B   Provide new avenues for cooperation with other divisions, especially within _____.

9

DEFINING AN OPPORTUNITY AREA FOR GROWTH

After setting the criteria for the ideal new product for your company, you may be inclined to try to meet these criteria, in workmanlike manner, as quickly as possible. That approach may work—if you're lucky, and if the criteria are truly innovation-sparking. But good, practicable, marketable new-product ideas usually don't present themselves quite that readily.

After you've used your ace up your sleeve (the 10 or 20 new-product ideas that you had already thought of and were just waiting for the proper time to present), and after you have invited others in the company to submit their best new-product ideas, and after you have left your transom open hoping the perfect idea would come over it and fall on you (one chemicals company I worked with actually solicited ideas for new products by advertising)—then where do you go?

If you sit passively by, waiting to react to ideas presented to you, you're going to get a lot of junk, a lot of new-product ideas that somehow miss the mark. They just don't fit your criteria, for one reason or another. The passive stance usually doesn't work.

Your criteria tell you what's right for your company. Now you're looking for what's right for the market, within that framework. So, if you resolve to take the initiative in generating new-product concepts that are on target, which direction should you take? A shotgun approach—scattering your shots all over the place—will certainly produce a low return for the effort expended. The world's pretty big, diverse, and complex. And it's changing rapidly these days.

Fortunately, the world does change! Who would want the job of trying to come up with a perfect new product in a *static* world? Things have a way of reaching a state of equilibrium over time. Problems get solved or disappear; needs eventually are filled. If the world stayed the same, or changed only sluggishly, it would be pretty tough to find new-product needs that haven't already been met. You've got to catch new needs and product opportunities on the rise.

The focus of your creative efforts, or the broad "envelope of opportunities" that will yield the greatest number of hits on your criteria "target," will be a moving, changing market area subject to new influences, new relationships among the parts, recent or repeated disruptions of the traditional way.

After all, the new product you ultimately develop will be introduced two or three years from now—not in today's market—even if you start immediately. On average, that's how long it takes to design, develop, and plan the introduction of a new product. Therefore, your focus, or area of concentration, must have a definite future orientation: what *will be*, not what is now or has been.

The all-important second step in the Strategic Innovation Process is finding this "opportunity area" for your company, based on current trends in the marketplace. You can then focus your efforts on achieving the company's growth objectives. The following guidelines will help make your new-product development efforts more productive.

Disequilibria

Search for change. And the more sudden those changes, the more likely you are to beat your competitors to the punch. If there is a change or discontinuity of some kind in the outside world, while your industry remains relatively static (in the short run), you have an opportunity to take positive action.

Relevant Trends

Look for opportunity areas in the outside world by identifying trends that are relevant to the criteria you have established. At any given time, there are scores of trends and countertrends—economic, regulatory, technological, social, "institutional"—that may present opportunities for your company. The procedure is simply to find several of these trends that can reasonably be combined and, voilà, you have a good, solid focus for your new-product development efforts.

Sources of Trend Intelligence

The print media—newspapers, general business magazines, trade magazines, newsletters, digests—provide an excellent view of what's going on in fields that may be related to your new-product criteria. Editors and news analysts receive bits of information from many sources; and they earn their living by synthesizing these fragments, detecting patterns, and drawing conclusions.

There are firms that specialize in performing trend studies and gathering primary data that could be useful to you.

Specialists who have broad exposure to changes in their particular fields are also valuable sources of information. Trade associations can be useful in tracking down these people.

Seek the advice of the highest-level people you can find. Chief executive officers are usually concerned more with the future than with day-to-day operations. Thus they make it their business to be aware of what's coming so they can position their firms accordingly.

People with responsibilities that call for a great deal of contact with others in a given industry accumulate the kind of information that can help identify trends. Purchasing agents, independent consultants, salesmen, stock analysts, advertising executives, and other "bees that flit from flower to flower" are excellent sources of trend intelligence.

A Dual, Interactive Approach

How do you get there? You can arrive at your opportunity area by identifying and combining a number of related trends that suggest specific "vehicles for expansion"—new products to be developed. But you can also go the other direction: if you come up with a couple of lucky hits (that is, new-product concepts that appear to have potential for meeting your criteria), you can step back and see what they have in common—and that can become the focal point, to ensure the efficiency of your further search. You can go either way: general to specifics, or specifics to general.

Testability

If the opportunity area is a good one, it should reveal, by itself, ideal entry points. Vehicles for expansion into the field that appear to have possibilities do not "earn points" simply because they fall within your opportunity area. They have value only if they appear to have potential for meeting your criteria. The fit of the product concepts to the target criteria is the goal, and the opportunity area is simply the means to get there.

Optimum Size

The reason for finding an opportunity area in the first place is to reduce the problem to manageable proportions. At the same time, the opportunity area should serve as a large enough "bucket" to hold a number (100?) of specific new-product possibilities. Don't focus too tight; leave some room to operate. At this initial point, the widest practical scope is called for, to identify possible expansion vehicles. As you continue downstream and generate or uncover specific "possibilities," you can then zero in on others that exhibit characteristics similar to those that have passed muster.

Any "Adequate" Focus Will Do

Keep in mind, there is not just one "perfect" opportunity area that will be useful in meeting the criteria you've established. A *number* of strategies may be adequate for your purpose, and any one of them could serve your ends. It's sometimes difficult to settle on one area of concentration and walk away from others that hold promise. In going in one direction, you are automatically not going in any other direction. But you must make a choice if progress is to be made.

Tally Ho!

A good opportunity area will inherently generate enthusiasm for the hunt. It will be fun, unique, exciting! (An SIC code would be anathema!) The conception of, or search for, the "ideal" new business/product line within the opportunity area should be adventurous. Find a forest you can enjoy hunting in!

SUMMARY

Remember, the first step in a rational new-product expansion plan is to define the characteristics of the "animal" you are hunting for, in terms of your company's growth objectives and the unique, leverageable assets that give it a particular advantage in the marketplace.

The second step—delineating a focus—is crucial. Once you have defined your criteria, you must not be distracted by "silver platter" business opportunities brought to you by others. You must take the initiative rather than adopting a comfortable, waiting posture. You must develop a hunting strategy.

There are so many diverse business opportunities—for *someone* out there—that it's hard to know where to start. More to the

point, it's hard to know when to stop. You could look under rocks forever, searching for the perfect opportunity. There are any number of attractive possibilities.

So the only answer is to embrace the self-discipline of adopting a focus—a broad, but not too broad, area of concentration. You must carve out a part of the total universe of possibilities. And the opportunity area you choose must be based on current trends and discontinuities that are relevant to your company's unique capabilities at this point in time.

10

THE
INNOVATION
SESSION

When a company needs a new-product concept or a new market-ing strategy, sometimes the person responsible for coming up with it tries *brainstorming*. Sometimes it works, and sometimes it doesn't.

The Innovation Session I'm going to describe below has its roots in brainstorming, but its success is mainly attributable to the ways in which it differs from brainstorming. The process always delivers a *number* of useful new ideas.

Have you ever participated in a conventional brainstorming session or watched one take place? What happens is probably something like this:

The guy with responsibility for solving the problem decides to "brainstorm" it. So he picks the "smartest" ten people in the department and informs them, by phone or memo, of the time, the date, and the topic of the meeting. He also tells them the place—which is the conference room down the hall.

Everybody files into the room and sits next to his pal—or in the same chair he sat in at the last meeting—at the long, rectangular conference table.

The meeting starts. The chairman says, "We want to do a little brainstorming here, and you remember the rule: 'Anything goes. No criticizing or putting down anyone else's idea. Just say anything that comes into your head.' Now here's the problem." A thorough explanation is followed by questions and answers. The boundaries and constraints are clearly laid out—what can't be done and what has already been tried.

The brainstorming on the problem proceeds and the recording secretary takes notes. After a couple of hours, during which time a lot of suggestions are contributed (more by some than by others), the five o'clock whistle blows. The chairman thanks everyone, and they all go home.

Next day, the recording secretary types up the minutes of the meeting. The guy with the problem may find a few new ideas that have potential merit. He turns them over to the appropriate subordinate for "further investigation." And so it goes.

BEYOND BRAINSTORMING

A few simple (and not so simple) changes in the procedure transform brainstorming into a highly productive Innovation Session. These changes didn't happen all at once. The process, as it now exists, is the result of development over the past ten years—of adding, modifying, eliminating, and improving.

First, there are some easy, mechanical changes you should make in order to increase the productiveness of your efforts to come up with new ideas.

◇ Hold the session off premises, not inside the walls of the corporation (which seems to be organized to *prevent* creativity). Certainly, don't conduct the creative session in the same room where other kinds of meetings—decision meetings, presentations, consensus development, committee meetings, and so on—are commonly held.

◇ Get yourself a *round* table. No head, no foot, no respective "positions." Round!

◇ Provide facilities for visual exposition. Flip charts, blackboards, places to hang and mount things—visual stimuli.

◇ Wire the room, so you can tape-record the session and catch everything.

◇ Hold the session in the morning, first thing. That's important. Any day but Monday.

◇ The leader should be skilled and experienced in running creative sessions. The executive with responsibility for solving the problem or coming up with the new product, is *not* the one to lead the session, unless he also possesses these skills.

◇ The leader should have a sidekick, an assistant or "facilitator." Their roles are different. The leader is responsible for driving the session and maintaining "pace," whereas the facilitator plays a subsidiary role, encouraging and supporting the individual contributor. (See Chapter 12.)

◇ Friends should not sit beside each other. The leader sits nearest the door. The facilitator sits opposite him at the other side of the table.

◇ In addition to the leader and facilitator, there should be *six* participants in the session (plus or minus one). Fewer than five is below critical mass; more than seven makes the group a crowd, and you'll "lose" some contributors.

◇ Participants should be provided, *in advance* (not during the beginning of the session), with carefully selected and controlled information designed to encourage and aid them in doing their homework beforehand.

◇ The leader introduces each participant, citing his background and its relevance to the task at hand. Everyone there is equally (and very) important.

◇ The leader opens the session by instructing the participants in the rules of the game. There is more than the "one rule of brainstorming." There are nine more for a productive Innovation Session. (See Table 2.)

◇ Use creative techniques. There are more than a hundred proven creative techniques in the literature. It's a science. They've been developed and tested by psychologists, academicians, and practitioners in the field. Creative techniques serve as a tool to stimulate creative thinking. You might use up to 20 of them, depending on the purpose of the session. (See Chapter 12.)

These changes are easy. They are things you can and should do to make your brainstorming sessions more productive.

We will deal with the preparation for and conduct of an Innovation Session in subsequent chapters. The balance of this chap-

Table 2. Guidelines for a productive innovation session.

RULE	CAVEAT
1. There are a *number* of "right" answers.	1. Don't seek "the" answer.
2. You have a piece of a lot of "right" answers. Say your piece.	2. Don't be shy.
3. Others have other pieces. Listen, and let them have their say. "Build on." Respond.	3. Don't dismiss or ignore others' contributions.
4. Stay positive! Support, modify, improve.	4. Don't criticize or shoot down.
5. Keep moving! Seek quantity, variety!	5. Don't dwell. Don't be boring!
6. Take a lead off base. Try way out!	6. Don't be constrained by convention.
7. Talk to the subject, not to a person.	7. Don't subgroup—don't whisper to your neighbor.
8. One at a time.	8. Don't interrupt.
9. Stay loose. Relax. Enjoy.	9. Don't be "careful" or cover your flank.
10. Keep punching! Hang in!	10. Don't shoot all your bullets and give up.

ter will be devoted to the selection of outside experts to participate in an Innovation Session.

SELECTION OF PARTICIPANTS IN AN INNOVATION SESSION

The task force approach is based on two assumptions. The first is that you don't know, for sure, the kind of expertise (discipline/education/technology/experience) needed for the solution. If you did, you'd have a "nonproblem" and could simply hire the world's greatest consultant in that field to give you the answer.

The second assumption is that the world today is quite different from what it was 100 years ago, or even 35 years ago. The world has been dramatically altered by what has been called the "technology explosion." How many normal appurtenances of everyday life—beginning with the electric light and the telephone—can you name that didn't exist over a century ago? What new technologies have affected your own industry since World War II? In the past ten years? These technological developments are a great credit to the small companies and independent inventors who were responsible for them. But, at the same time, they add to the difficulty of inventing and discovering in today's world: there is simply too much technology for any one person to absorb it all.

In short, what I'm saying is that more than likely you can't and don't know who's got the answer. What's more, nobody's got it all.

If you invite the six "smartest" people from one department (say, sales) to an Innovation Session, you may think you have six people in the room, but you don't. You have one salesman, six times. The other problem is that they may be knowledgeable, but not particularly creative—or they may just be vocal! What you need is both creativity and knowledge.

With respect to creativity, there are four kinds of people in the world. "Alpha" people are the sparks. They spew raw ideas out, one after another, all over. "Beta" people are the responders. They react and develop and vary and build on the ideas of others. "Gamma" people shake down and convert ideas to practical application. They provide the transition from concept to product. "Delta" people come along a year or so later and make the minor modifications and refinements that will constitute the next "new, improved" model.

Look for mostly Alphas and Betas to participate in Innovation Sessions. They contribute the first and greatest measure to the final, perfected new product.

With respect to knowledge, the participants should possess background and experience relevant to the potential solution. They should, specifically, *not* be totally knowledgeable about the problem. That would only hinder them, putting them in the same box as the manager responsible for coming up with the new product. You want fresh perspectives brought to bear on the task. Employees within the company simply know too much. They know all the things you've tried before, and all the reasons that something new will never work.

The responsible executives within the company can evaluate the *results* of the creative efforts afterward. They can select the good new-product ideas from all the concepts proposed by the outsiders.

When Alex Osborne began experimenting with brainstorming in the 1930s, he recognized that every new idea is a combination of known elements in a different relationship. Any single cranium holds only so many "known elements" in the folds and wrinkles of the cortex. A person can apply his imagination only to his "knowns." He has only so much to work with.

Osborne's insight was to link *several* heads, full of different, relevant "known elements," via the synaptic analog of the "electricity" of personal interaction. Our insight has been to build and maintain a Brain Bank of experts from all over the country. They are on call to participate in our Innovation Sessions when and as their particular perspectives (background and specialized experience) seem to represent, in our judgment, a potential contribution to solving the problem at hand.

There is another dimension that makes this approach more appropriate—even necessary—today. In the past 40 years, knowledge has grown explosively. The total body of knowledge is now doubling about every ten years, and that rate has been constant for a considerable period of time. If we work backward, then, half our present stock of information was available in 1971, one-quarter in 1961, one-eighth in 1951, and one-sixteenth in 1941. In other words, about 94 percent of everything we know now has come along in the past 40 years. It is now patently impossible for any single person to fully comprehend a problem of any breadth by reading a few books in the field—as was the case when Osborne developed brainstorming in the 1930's. So you just *have* to adopt a "gang" approach.

Now let's choose the members of your ad hoc task force.

The first step is to break down the problem into six component parts, or rather into six key aspects to which different disciplines, educational backgrounds, technologies, or experiences appear to relate. Next, "abstract" each discipline by asking yourself the following questions: (1) Where is this technology being used in combination with other technologies? (2) Where is it being dealt with on a broader theoretical level? (3) Where is it being employed for different but analogous purposes? (4) Where is it likely to have exposure to a broad range of applications?

This sort of analysis will lead you to the six experts you should invite to your Innovation Session. This group will be able to suggest technology-transfer possibilities, provide fresh insights from perspectives that are different from your own, and (very important) suggest new, creative approaches.

No single expert should be relied on to come up with the whole answer. But even if I'm wrong in that assumption, and one line of expertise does, in fact, yield the answer, this approach is still valid. Under such circumstances, it can be looked upon as a means of identifying the right source through intelligent shot-gunning.

What kinds of outside experts should you invite to your Innovation Session? Let me suggest some categories: professors, consulting engineers, marketing consultants, operating executives, editors of trade magazines, government experts, government administrators, retirees, independent professionals. Anyone is "fair game" to invite to an Innovation Session if his background and special perspective, in your judgment, are relevant to the task. There are a lot of strange ways to make a living, a lot of geniuses in their fields. And there are a great many cooperative, enthusiastic people out there who would be delighted to engage in some intellectual calisthenics. Try inviting them to participate in your brainstorming sessions. You'll see.

On the following pages are some examples of the backgrounds of participants in Innovation Sessions that we recently conducted for specific companies. The outside experts drawn together for Company X were asked to "come up with a lot of new packaging products for the fast-food restaurant market." Their task is laid out by the first Briefing Document at the end of Chapter 11.

The experts assembled for Company Y were asked to "conceive strategies for starting the new business" of managing demonstration projects for industry. They were briefed for their task by the second Briefing Document at the end of Chapter 11.

Company Z was seeking new high-technology growth businesses it could enter by acquisition of a medium-size firm.

INNOVATION SESSION X

Ph.D. Physicist. Currently with a Princeton-based Defense Department think tank; formerly a senior research scientist with the Linde Division of Union Carbide. Expertise includes heat transfer, combustion processes, solar collector design, and process instrumentation.

Director of Market Research and Development for one of the nation's largest packaging materials/components manufacturers. He has had more than 20 years' experience in the development, marketing, and sale of many of this company's innovative products and systems.

Ph.D. Food Scientist and Professor Emeritus at Cornell University (28 years). Expansive knowledge of food processing, preparation, and the development of meal service systems. Directed the design of the Boeing 747 kitchen and the Apollo capsule food system. Also has had 13 years' industrial experience as a food technologist for Coca-Cola, Heinz, and other companies.

Industrial Designer. Principal of a successful product development and engineering company. Did extensive design and development work on AMF's fully automated fast-food restaurant system.

Consumer Marketing "Pro." Publisher of the "Dining Out" magazines; formerly Senior Vice President of Gould Associates, a well-known package design firm; previously creative director of several large advertising agencies and a product manager for Procter & Gamble. A savvy, creative individual, he is well acquainted with the needs and inner workings of the fast-food industry.

President of a Connecticut-based advertising agency. Formerly a vice president of creative services for Young & Rubicam. Heavy experience in packaged goods.

INNOVATION SESSION Y

Former Undersecretary of Department of Energy. Currently President of Energy Clinic, Inc., a management consulting firm specializing in energy conservation.

President of Wire and Cable Division of Phelps Dodge. Responsible for utility, industrial, and construction markets; engineered products; and research and development, including contract research.

Consulting Physicist. Formerly Director of Research for General Time Corp. and Remington Rand. Ph.D. from Harvard in physics and communications engineering.

Manager of Science Policy Studies, Office of Public Sector Programs, at the American Association for the Advancement of Science. Responsible for preparation of Five-Year Outlook for Science and Technology.

President of Industrial Research Institute Corporation. Responsible for study with Department of Commerce on cooperative research with private sector. IRI has membership of 250 companies seeking to improve research and development operations. Formerly Director of Research for Monsanto.

Executive Director of Manufacturing Studies Board at National Academy of Sciences. Responsible for providing staff support for task force of experts working on policy analysis for the federal government with regard to manufacturing industries.

INNOVATION SESSION Z

Director of Marketing and Business Strategy for a major diversified manufacturing corporation. Responsibilities include mergers, acquisitions, and divestitures, new-product development and diversification programs, and corporate strategic planning. A Harvard MBA, he has 20 years' experience in fostering corporate growth through product development, diversification, and acquisition programs.

Senior Vice President for a major management consulting firm responsible for their technology transfer and technology search activities. A graduate chemical engineer, he worked with General Electric and THIOKOL in product development. With more than ten years in technology transfer, he is conversant with technical developments and trends in R&D in a wide variety of industries.

Program Director of a quasi public corporation whose charter is to transfer technology from industry to the municipal sector. His responsibilities include the coordination of technology applications teams with the activities of User Requirement Committees, made up of elected officials and municipal managers. Some of the areas in which his group has been involved include fire fighting, telecommunications, energy conservation, infra-structure maintenance (roads, bridges, tunnels, pipelines), waste treatment, and emergency medical services.

Former Director of Marketing for a major chemicals corporation and for the Plastics Division of General Electric. Over 30 years' experience in product and market development and corporate strategic planning. His current activities as a private management consultant have focused on international·business development for the rubber and plastics industry.

Former Director of Planning and Technology Management for a major pharmaceuticals manufacturer. A chemical E./P.E., he is actively involved in organizations dedicated to the advancement of planning and management techniques, is a senior editor of *Planning Review*, and is Associate Professor of Management at Hofstra University. As a result of his experience and his current activities as a management consultant, he has an excellent perspective on potential growth opportunities for the chemicals industry.

11

PREPARING
FOR AN
INNOVATION SESSION:
THE BRIEFING DOCUMENT

An Innovation Session is very much like the Big Game—or a final exam. It is a one-chance opportunity to do your best. You have a limited period of time from start to finish to do it, and you will do your best only if you prepare yourself in advance.

During the session itself, you are under the gun, because the human brain can operate at peak energy level—approaching its maximum processing capacity of 27 bits of information per second—for only three or four hours before becoming exhausted. So you certainly don't want to blow any of that precious time explaining what the problem is and fielding questions.

Well in advance of the Innovation Session, the participants should begin doing their homework. As someone so aptly put it, "Chance favors the prepared mind." So select a few fresh minds and prepare them, brief them, without contaminating their perspective. A carefully designed Briefing Document—something they can study and mull over—should be prepared and forwarded to each expert approximately ten days before the Innovation Session. It should be designed to do the job.

What *is* the job of the Briefing Document? I'll tell you what it's *not:* it's not a complete and factual report conveying accurate information. That is not your purpose, to "convey information." The Briefing Document is purely a creative tool. More precisely, it is an instrument designed to elicit creative insights into a specific, defined problem.

Let me tell you something else it is not: it's not a literary tour de force, by any means. It will never receive a number from the Library of Congress; it will never be reviewed by a disinterested critic. It will be reviewed, studied, and worked on only by those directly involved—those on whom it will work its effect: the stimulation of new ideas that are relevant to the task at hand. Again, it's a creative tool, a device to encourage your experts to think along productive lines and come up with "interesting" suggestions.

A good Briefing Document is written *for* those who will act on it (and on whom it will act). It "talks" to those six outside experts, warming them to the task. That's the style.

GUIDELINES FOR PREPARING THE BRIEFING DOCUMENT

Below are some of the dos and don'ts—the guidelines and caveats—for preparing a Briefing Document. These are the "precepts to provoke percepts," if you will.

1. State the objective up front, first thing. Make that the title. What do you want the experts-in-their-field to do? Develop strategies? Conceive new products? Identify different markets? Tell them exactly what their task is. Not only in the beginning, but repeatedly throughout the document. End with that clear charge!

2. Put the hypothesis to bed. Give a brief, plausible rationale,

followed by the report of management's decision on the matter. "Here are the facts. This is the background. The company has decided it wants _____." Be positive. Don't allow room for argument with the hypothesis. Get the starting point behind you!

3. Feed people useful information, and only useful information. Don't tell them all you know. Some data are simply irrelevant to the task (which is to come up with new ideas, not to analyze and judge). And some information will inhibit rather than stimulate ideas. It is counterproductive to the creative process to report all the things that have been tried and that won't work. If you tell the outside experts all you know, you will put them in the same box you are in. Parcel out only that which will aid progress. Nobody makes progress by *not* doing something!

4. Qualifying squelches creativity. Don't focus your questions too tightly. Leave some room for some unanticipated responses. If you are looking for answers, if you don't know all the answers, maybe you shouldn't be too sure of yourself, too sure you have the exactly right question. You're after *quantity* of ideas; you can build in the quality later. It is impossible to think up a large number of only good ideas. (Besides, who is the judge of what's good?) Take anything you can get!

5. The mind has a mind of its own. At any given moment, the mind may be in any one of three dominant modes: perception, processing, or preparing for transmission. And that is the typical sequence of modes. So when you write the Briefing Document, try to give the reader something to perceive, an opportunity to process what has been perceived—a chance to chew on it—and some space to respond or transmit a reaction. Try to get in sync with the reader's mind.

6. The mind follows its own trails at its own pace. Both direction and speed vary from person to person, but you can provide a loose lead. A lead, not a tether. And let people's minds wander

where they will, along the wide trails you're traversing. The mind can go in only one direction at once, so don't jerk it around. Dwell on one aspect of the problem for a little while; then move on to the next related area and play around there. Get your stuff together and deal with one topic at a time.

7. Ask questions, lots of questions, the kinds of questions germane to the task, which you have reason to believe your experts can answer. In preparing the Briefing Document, you are writing to and for the diverse group of experts whose backgrounds you know. They are each knowledgeable in the subject area, albeit from different perspectives. Ask them what they know. (In the process of writing the document, you may find that an additional field of expertise may be useful for dealing with some of the questions posed. If that is the case, recruit an expert in the new field as well. You write for the experts, and you recruit for the document—it's an interactive process.) In framing your questions, you should ask only what you want to know, or what will lead you there. Broad, general questions will yield broad, general answers. If that's what you want, fine. If not, get down to the nits. Responses to questions will be in kind.

8. Utilize creative techniques—completing lists, filling in blanks, suggesting relationships. Very productive! Get people started by offering examples of your own as bait. Make it easy, and fun. Don't overpower the experts with too-good answers. That may be defeating. It doesn't hurt to inject a little humor into the document, to offer a touch of the bizarre or the ridiculous. Loosen up!

9. Nobody puts anything in a full box! Leave your questions and lists open-ended. Never, but never, use "etc." "Etc." means "There are lots of others; I know all of them. What's more, I'm not the least bit interested in that whole subject, so let's move on." It's a high-handed squelch. Don't shut off subjects unless you mean to. The Briefing Document is a tool to be worked with by others. It is not a monograph. It should serve as a forum for

two-way communication. Your goal is to enlist active participation in thinking—thinking about the subject. By writing the document, you just went first!

10. Don't be afraid to go on for 10 or 12 pages. Involve the reader. Expect answers. Require reactive involvement. Charge the experts with the responsibility of coming up with the best they can offer, from their individual perspectives and those of their colleagues, in preparation for the Innovation Session. Both Protestants and Catholics enjoy hard work!

Two good examples of Briefing Documents, on widely different subjects, appear at the end of the chapter. The first was written by Robert Benchley, Jr., and the other by Robert Steigerwald. I know they are good Briefing Documents because, as a practical matter, they worked: they elicited many relevant ideas and insights from the experts participating in the respective Innovation Sessions. Remember, *any* creative problem can be the subject of a good Briefing Document, and *anyone* (with a little practice) can write one.

THE INSIDER-OUTSIDER RELATIONSHIP

There are a couple of differences between Briefing Documents prepared by independent consultants and those prepared by "insiders" who represent their company.

First, in "putting the hypothesis to bed," you'll note that independent consultants never clearly identify "the client." That is done purposefully, to avoid contaminating the perspective of the outside experts. If someone came right out and said, for example, that Otis Elevator was looking for new-product ideas, the only thing that some people would come up with are things that go up and down—the obvious stuff that Otis Elevator is already making or has already thought of. But Otis would be looking for something new. So it helps to give your outside experts a *tabula rasa*.

As an "insider" preparing a Briefing Document, you have to

find a way to develop a plausible scenario that will elicit the kinds of ideas you want. You get no points for accuracy or for completeness in this game. You get points only for delivering solid new-product concepts.

How can you prepare the outside experts without giving away too much? Maybe you can refer to some obscure overseas division of your company. Or perhaps you can indicate that your firm is contemplating an acquisition, or a joint venture with another company, and that everything must be kept "highly confidential." All you need do is find some pretext to avoid supplying definitive answers to questions and to prevent second-guessing and evaluation by the experts. Remember, you're looking for fresh ideas and starting points, not enunciations of conventional wisdom. So take charge. Do it your way. Feign ignorance; hide under the cloak of confidentiality. Whatever works.

Another problem you may run into, in conducting the Innovation Session as a representative of the company, is that you may be forced into the role of on-the-spot evaluator. The outside experts will be looking to you for acceptance and approval of their suggestions. In that case, you may be strongly tempted to reject some ideas. That sort of climate violates the cardinal rule of group creativity: "Anything goes." You are there not to arrive at "the" solution, or to get the "right" new-product concepts, but rather to generate the *maximum number of relevant possibilities*. That may seem a fine distinction, but it makes all the difference in whether the group is in a creative mode or a judgmental mode—and the volume of ideas generated will vary accordingly.

BRIEFING DOCUMENT 1

SESSION DATE

Tuesday, September 19, 1978
9:00 A.M.–Noon

SESSION OBJECTIVE

To come up with a lot of new ways to make disposable packaging work for the fast-food restaurant market.

INTRODUCTION

Our client, a small-size Scandinavian packaging company, is well known for its imaginative use of packaging for all kinds of goods. All kinds, that is, except foods. The one exception is the Tetrahedron you may have seen some airlines use to hold milk and other liquids. Smart!

The efforts in Europe have been so successful that it has been decided to use the company's expertise on a real giant—the American fast-food restaurant market.

We have been hired to implement the company's efforts by conceiving all the new ways in which the pedestrian disposable package can be made to give readily perceived benefits to the consumer and/or the fast-food restaurant operator.

TASK

The task of this session, therefore, is to come up with a lot of new ways to make disposable packaging work for the fast-food restaurant market *by adding benefits.*

MORE ON THE CLIENT

Owing to recent overseas acquisitions, our client is now able to produce disposable packaging using *all* the standard materials: paper, paper-board, plastic, foam, film, and foil. It can also combine these materials or manipulate them to adjust to any desired food "climate."

What kind of "climate" would keep a Fast Food happy?

Hamburger	Hot
French fries	Nongreasy
Shake	Icy
Fried chicken	Southern
(You name a few)	

How could you do this by combining materials?

Line a paperboard box with foam to insulate?

Yes, but what *else*? _____

Here are some more:

Onion rings	_____
Fish sandwiches	_____
Mexican foods	_____
Soups	Steamy

BACK TO WORK

At this point, we're not looking for any wild new technologies; we just want a lot of new tactics, packaging systems, or design features (that might be added to a known package). Actually, our client would be very pleased if we came up with a "thing" that was the progenitor of a whole new family of packages.

If you were a "thing," how would *you* come up with a whole new family?

_____   _____

_____   _____

ABOUT THE MARKET

A few pithy observations may help us put our job into sharper focus. A fast-food restaurant is just that; it is *fast!* The food must be prepared and served in one minute or less. And a "disposable package" is just that way too; it is the "vehicle" on which the food is transported from the serving area to the general vicinity of the customer's mouth, there to be eaten. Fast! It is then immediately disposed of. Out with it!

During these few precious minutes of useful life, the "disposable" can be very busy. If it's any good at all, it must be obedient, neat, and useful to the operator, to the food, and to the customer. And that's where we come in. We want to come up with a lot of new ways to make

"SMART" PACKAGES

If you were a "smart" package, what would you do for the food?

How

Protect?	_____
Carry?	_____
Insulate?	_____

Name some more. _____   _____

_____   _____

How about some exothermic stuff in a take-out carton that would rewarm the food later on?

No? OK, *you* come up with a couple.

If you were a "smart" package, what would you be for the restaurant operator?

How

Easy to fill?	_____
Strong?	Carbon fibers
Light?	Microencapsulated helium
Adjustable?	Accordian
Look bigger?	Magnifier in lid
Food-fitting?	Custom partitions
Money-saving?	_____

Go on, name some more.

_____   _____

_____   _____

_____   _____

_____   _____

How about an elasticized pop-up box—ships flat for saving valuable storage space, pops up for fast filling?

What would you do for the customer to prevent:

	How
Spilling?	High sides
Messy fingers?	Finger bowl
Tipping?	"No Tipping Allowed" sign
Slopping?	_____
Leaking?	_____
More, please.	

_____   _____

_____   _____

Look down the list of problems/needs and try to come up with "smart" packages to answer/fill them.

Fast-Food Problems/Needs

Minimize storage space	(Let's build a nest.)
Minimize food waste	(Package is "smart" enough to control portion size.)
Keep hot food hot	(A package that allows foods with good heat retention—like apple pie—to warm food with poor heat retention, like french fries. How?)
Messy fingers	(A "handywipe" integrated into the package?)

Make the food more appealing and attractive, or just plain MORE	(Via shape, color, graphics, a magnifying glass?)
Carton either too big or too small	(A one-size-fits-all package made of Spandex; a girdle for your onion rings or panty hose for your fries.)
Foods (especially some ethnics) run together	
Disposables that have the strength of nondisposables	(Apply structural engineering here.)
Let steam out, keep heat in	(How?)
Fries fall out of ordinary bag	(What's your bag—ugh!)
Fish or chicken get crushed in the bottom of a pail	
Onions must be hand-counted and put into a bag—you can't use a scoop	(Do you know how the game of Quoits might apply here?)
Salads need a distinctly new container/package—not a paper bowl	

BACK TO MARKET

In the last ten years the fast-food restaurant market has grown to a $20 billion industry, but its problems have grown right along with it. In order to keep even it must continue to increase *overall* profits and reduce *overall* costs.

Now $20 billion is a lot of dollars, but it's also a lot of individual servings—and at *one* minute per serving, who can guess how many mils/per cubic inch/per bite/per package we're talking about? It's microscopic! Luckily, we're not after a cheap disposable package, we're after a lot of "smart" packaging systems that can increase overall profits in many different ways.

Say, for instance, we spend a few cents to make a "smart" paper bag. And say this bag is so smart that it allows the customer to carry a high-profit drink in the *same* hand. And say that ploy raises the price of the *average* meal check by 20¢.

F-a-a-an-tastic!

Look over the following list of nonpackaging things and see if they suggest a new "smart" package.

Nondisposable —Nonpackaging "Things"

To Hold Something	To cover, or go under
Suitcase	Trivet
Oven	Roof
Refrigerator	Scarf
Crib	Canopy
Hat box	Mattress
Pullstring bag	Paint
Igloo	Slipcover
Gourd	Rug
Tank	Bib
Pocket	Hat
Vault	Antimacassar

How about some more "things" that protect from damage, heat, cold, wet, fire?

Umbrella	Wet suit
Cushion	Shade
Dark glasses	

How does Mother Nature handle it?

Egg shell	"Fur coat"
Kangaroo pouch	Skin
Feathers	Scales
Honeycomb	Spines
Banana	Cocoon

FINALE

After you have read this document once or twice, please visit your local fast-food restaurant, on us, with document and a $5 bill in hand. Look at the customers. Are they unhappy about anything? Make a note.

Look at the employees. Does anything seem to be slowing them down? Make a note. Ask the restaurant operator to show you his kitchen, his storage area. Be a little nosy—ask some questions. And make some notes. Then come home and really go to work!

Fill out as many of the enclosed cards as you can with great ideas— eight, nine? Use some more for pretty good ideas, even *silly* ones (we love 'em).

BRIEFING DOCUMENT 2

SESSION DATE

Tuesday, March 4, 1980
9:00 A.M. to 12:00 Noon
Blue Room, Plaza Hotel
Fifth Ave. at 59th Street
New York City

SESSION OBJECTIVE

To conceive strategies for "growing" a new business.

INTRODUCTION

> Management of Complex, Technologically Challenging Development or Demonstration Projects for Industry

This is the charter for a new business venture that our client has recently undertaken.

Our client is a major, multidivisional corporation, widely recognized for its large, highly effective research and development organization.

Over the years it has built up a successful track record in (among many other endeavors) the management of development projects and demonstration facilities for the federal government. The company suspects that there is an untapped market for these services in the industrial sector (state and local governments included, by the client's definition) and has asked us to help develop this business.

Our task in this session will be to conceive strategies for penetrating and developing the market for IOCOs—*I*ndustry *O*wned–*C*ontractor *O*perated development and demonstration projects and facilities.

THE IDEAL PROJECT

There are some basic attributes that a potential new project for our client must possess:

Complexity:

The project or facility must require the assembly and management of many individuals, subcontractors, and so on. For example, one project our client is currently managing for the federal government requires a staff of 100 (half were recruited specifically for this task) overseeing the efforts of some 25 subcontractors. This is in keeping with the modus operandi that characterizes our client's other operations and that is a major strength. *Something to keep in mind:* the complexity of a project can also come, in part, from having a *number of owners* — for example, a consortium of firms each supplying partial funding and sharing in the results.

Technological Challenge:

Our client has one of the nation's premiere research and development organizations. Its strength lies in the management and successful carry-through of high-technology programs in a wide variety of scientific and engineering disciplines. The advantage over potential competition would come as a result of this strength; the award of contracts to our client will depend on it. Consequently, in our conceptualization of growth strategies and in our identification of project opportunities, the theme of technological challenge must be very much in evidence.

Demonstration and Development:

The project that our client undertakes will be at the *postresearch stage.* The technology or technologies on which the project is based will be proved to the point where the end results of the application of that technology can be predicted with some certainty; costs, method of approach, scheduling, and the probability of achieving the goals of the program can be ascertained in advance with an acceptable level of accuracy.

Time Frame:

The needs of industry that will form the basis for the ideal demonstration or development project must be current—*now;* we're aiming for a contract award before the end of 1981.

DEVELOPING STRATEGIES AND IDENTIFYING OPPORTUNITIES

Much of what we come up with here will be the result of identifying needs in industry that could be met via a demonstration or development project managed by our client. Consider:

Productivity:

American industry's performance has been dismal and there is a real need for technology to boost productivity.

Government Regulation:

Compliance often requires the development of new processes that will not produce or that can clean up contaminants, or that can test facilities to ascertain and diminish risk to the public.

Geopolitical Stress:

Energy supplies and raw materials held hostage. Needed are alternative energy technologies, new processes to use less of "sensitive" materials, or new materials to replace them completely.

Economics:

Compliance with government regulations through technology places a burden on companies that cooperative ventures could ameliorate.

Complex Industrial Processes:

Some technologies in use are so complex and critical (dangerous) that there is a need for education and training of operating personnel (for example, in nuclear plant operations).

Emerging Technology:

A new technology may be the "answer to a maiden's prayer," but it may be too expensive for one company to develop. A consortium approach to development may be possible, though.

List some new technologies that you know about and which industries they will affect:

_____

_____

_____

_____

Are there some opportunities here for our client? (Please use the enclosed cards.)

Then, there are some possible growth strategies that can be developed with a bit of creativity. Consider:

Which industries have materials or processes in common? There may be a mix of diverse companies that use the same basic materials for totally different products. They could all benefit from new technology applied to the production of those materials.

For example: Suppose a new process had just been proved in the lab for producing high-alloy steel for 50 percent less than the existing process. It's easily conceivable that U.S. Steel, General Motors, and a major appliance manufacturer might be sold on funding a development/demonstration program.

Trace the flow of some basic materials or commodity fabricated products (like construction materials) and see if you can come up with some other examples:

_____

_____

_____

_____

All the companies within an industry share some needs in common. Following is a list of industries and a list of needs. Add to both and see if by fitting one list to the other you can identify an opportunity for our client.

Industries	Needs
Paper	Toxicological testing
Glass	Waste disposal
Steel	Energy conservation
Rubber	Product liability testing
Machine tools	Process innovation
Semiconductors	New electronics technology
Utilities	New materials
Petroleum	Worker/operator training
Coal	"Taming" a new technology
_____	_____
_____	_____
_____	_____
_____	_____

Some examples of potential projects to stimulate your thinking:

—A full-scale demonstration facility for an advanced energy storage technology.

—A space industrialization development project, such as for manufacturing ultrapure ceramics or semiconductors in orbit.

—A center for the development of procedures for handling and disposing of hazardous materials.

—A center for the nondestructive testing of high-pressure valves used in the electric power industry.

—A center for training nuclear reactor operating personnel.

—An arctic petroleum operations engineering laboratory to develop techniques of oil spill prevention, prediction of iceberg behavior, crew training. (*Hint:* What other adverse environments have industries been forced to work in because of energy or raw material shortages, regulations, or other factors?)

—An industrial toxicological test facility.

—A regional facility for handling or disposing of hazardous waste material.

Finally, given the charter of our client's new venture as described in the first two pages, on whom would you make sales calls? On trade associations? Which ones? On many individual corporations or the leading company in a particular industry? Which ones?

If you were to undertake an advertising campaign, where would you advertise? What would you say?

IN SUMMARY

We are out to conceive strategies for developing the market for IOCOs. Please be sure to work this document through thoroughly, especially where we ask you to identify current industrial needs that require a technological fix.

Please record your thoughts and ideas on the enclosed cards. (One idea per card please!)

See you on the 4th!

12

CONDUCTING THE INNOVATION SESSION: THE LEADER'S FUNCTION

CREATIVITY VERSUS ANALYSIS

There are only two kinds of problems in the world—those that have only one correct solution and those that admit of a number of solutions, above some level of acceptability. The accountant is usually faced with problems of the former type (2 plus 3 should never equal 4.8). The engineer sees some of these same problems as well—problems that lend themselves to *analysis*, successive elimination of wrong answers, and subsequent proof.

On the other hand, the marketing manager faces problems that may admit of any number of strategies; the new-product designer can develop any number of products that will succeed. There is not just one right answer. These kinds of problems lend themselves to *creativity*. Such problems have an infinite number of wrong answers, but they also have *several* right answers.

In short, there are "analysis problems"—diving, bowling, and crew—and "creativity problems"—squash racquets, boxing, and cat-skinning generally. Any time you can express your problem as "What are all the ways I could . . . ?" you have a creativity problem. It's as simple as that.

With an analysis problem, the fewer misfires, the better. No value attaches to fumbling around before you get to *the* right answer. With a creativity problem, by contrast, the more options you generate, the better. The head of the class of 100 is probably superior to the head of the class of 10. The greater the universe from which the winner is selected, the more likely it is to be of higher quality.

Here are the keys to the kingdom. When you face a creativity problem, do not sit down with the objective of finding "the" answer. That will only force you into a judgmental, analytical mode of thinking. Rather, sit down with the goal of generating as many options as you can, in and around the target. That's the answer—it will be there somewhere.

New-product development is a creativity problem. At this point we'll assume you've found a way to go at it (a focus of effort). Now if you go out and recruit the best brains in the world relevant to various aspects of the potential solution (*not* aspects of the problem), and you bring them together in the same place, what have you got? You simply have the raw material from which acceptable solutions can be fabricated, that's all! You haven't pushed the "start" button. Nothing happens.

You have to find some way to "turn on" these outside experts. You have to "actuate" this brainpower to generate relevant options. How are you going to do that?

That is the responsibility of the leader of an Innovation Session. He must provide a "safe place"; he must help the participants perceive the elements of the problem, perhaps in a new light. He must be the catalyst to set in motion the cutting and fitting and trying of new combinations. The leader must also infuse "electricity" into the meeting to ensure pace. Finally, it is the leader's function to drive the Innovation Session, to make sure it goes in the right direction, and to orchestrate the participants' contribution and manage the group dynamics along the way.

CREATIVE TECHNIQUES

There are many classic, proven techniques for stimulating individual creativity and enhancing the creative productivity of groups. Creative thinking is a "science." It has all the earmarks of a science: a body of literature has built up on the subject of creative techniques—the terminology has standardized and an in-group jargon has developed. There are proponents of one approach over another; certain creative techniques bear the name of their originators. There are centers and institutions here and abroad devoted to the advancement of the art. Independent researchers in the field are scattered about the world. (I have personally traded notes with experts in Toronto, St. Louis, Long Island, Sharon, Dearborn, Greenboro, Berkeley, Buffalo, and Surrey, Bedford, and Cambridge, England. A summary of creative techniques is shown in Table 3. (See also the Selected Readings at the end of the book.)

Although there are scores of creative techniques, I arbitrarily lump all of them into three basic categories, depending on their primary purpose.

The Ego Protectors

A number of creativity exercises are *designed to protect the ego*—to help a person overcome his shyness and come out of his shell. They encourage him to say whatever occurs to him, to throw out to the group what's on the top of his head without fear of being laughed at or criticized or looking foolish. One such technique is called "key triggering." It involves subjecting the entire group to a common, medium-level tension by requiring each member to write down as many items he can think of that bear a certain characteristic. The leader demands an impossibly

Table 3. Summary of creative techniques.

NATURE OF PROBLEM	OUTPUT OR RESULT DESIRED	APPROPRIATE OPERATIONAL TECHNIQUE	COMMENTS AND EXPERIENCES
Problem is open-ended; problem is well defined; simple solution is sought; problem is easily understood; problem has more than one acceptable solution; participants are able and willing to freewheel and emphasize the positive.	One or more simple, feasible, creative solutions to a well-defined problem that is well understood.	Brainstorming Free association Heuristics	Methods are often restricted by biases and social inhibitions of one or more participants.
Problem is open-ended; problem is poorly defined; simple solution is sought; problem is not well understood; problem has more than one acceptable solution; participants are initially unable to freewheel and unable to emphasize the positive.	Analysis of faults, failure modes, things to be corrected in an area that may be incompletely understood.	Reverse brainstorming Edisonian method Kepner-Tregoe method	Methods are often useful starting points for other methods.
Problem is open-ended; problem is fairly well defined; a complex illogical solution may be sought; problem is fairly well understood; problem has one best solution; participants are able to emphasize the bizarre, analogize and emphasize the positive.	A far-out solution, that may be toned down if desired.	Synectics Bionics Inspired (big dream) approach Gordon method Buffalo method	Methods require skilled and trained participants for complete success; methods are good for areas where the technology is poorly defined.

Table 3. Summary of creative techniques (continued).

NATURE OF PROBLEM	OUTPUT OR RESULT DESIRED	APPROPRIATE OPERATIONAL TECHNIQUE	COMMENTS AND EXPERIENCES
Problem may not be open-ended; problem is fairly well defined; problem is not well understood; problem has many acceptable solutions; participants are able to work in the abstract.	A solution that cannot be visualized, conceptualized, or described before the sessions; the elaboration of concepts; dimensions or ideas for further refinement.	Gordon method Inspired (big dream) approach Synectics	Methods are fully dependent upon the skill of the leader; methods can be good where the technology is poorly defined; methods are good where participants would otherwise rush toward an obvious solution.
Problem need not be open-ended; problem is well defined; problem is well understood; problem has several acceptable solutions, but one best solution; participants are able to visualize combinations and attributes; attributes are well defined; combinations and variations are meaningful.	New combinations, forms, shapes, or means.	Checklists Attribute listing Morphological analysis Forced relationships Input–output technique	Methods are limited by ability of participants to visualize combinations; methods work best in well-defined, state-of-art technologies.

Problem may be either open- or closed-ended; problem is well defined; simple, logical solution is sought; one best solution is desired; the technology or discipline being studied is well known; a logical process may be followed to reach a solution; an algorithmic approach may be taken to solution.	A far-out solution is not desired; the bits and pieces of the problem are laying around, waiting to be properly assembled.	Input–output technique Buffalo method CNB (collective notebook) method SAMM (sequence-attribute/ modifications matrix) Value engineering Scientific method Heuristics Kepner-Tregoe method	Methods require that some participants be highly knowledgeable about the technology/discipline under study; group must be heterogeneous (some creative thinkers, some resident experts, some confronters); methods may be good starting points for other methods, such as synectics, Gordon method, and brainstorming.
Problem is closed-ended; problem is well defined; a best, logical solution is desired; an engineered solution that can be immediately put into effect is desired; the technology or discipline being studied is highly defined.	Only incremental change is sought, such as a change in form, type, or process.	Buffalo method CNB (collective notebook) method Value engineering Scientific method	Methods normally yield success because the problem is well defined and there is little uncertainty in recognizing an acceptable solution.

Courtesy of *Research Management* magazine.

large quantity within an impossibly short time, such as two minutes. At the end of the period, the leader calls time and, regardless of the results, compliments the group members on how well they did. This relieves the tension, and a bond has thus been formed among the members of the group as a result of their shared emotional experience.

Another ego protector, designed to eliminate "self-ness" among members of a group, is "role playing." Here the leader asks each person to make believe he is expert in a given field (other than his own). Members are then free to suggest ideas under the guise of their adopted role, rather than taking a position from the standpoint of their real identity. One step beyond that technique is "role reversal," in which members of the group *trade* roles for a while. This has the advantage of providing a knowledgeable sounding board for the naive (and sometimes very insightful) suggestions made by people who are not trapped by conventions of a given métier.

Another means of eliminating the fear of appearing foolish in a group (or, more accurately, of appearing conspicuous by virtue of one's relative foolishness as compared with the group norm) is a technique called "synectics." Here the leader places everyone in the group in the depths of foolishness to begin with by having them pretend that they *are* the item they are working on. For example, if you were a beer bottle and you wanted to be the best, most-respected little beer bottle in the world, what color would you be? Why, green, of course! And if you'd just spend some time being a doorknob it might help you and your fellow doorknobs design some new features into a lock. And not one of you will feel particularly ridiculous, because that's where you are all starting from.

The Perception Raisers

The second basic category of creative techniques are those *designed to facilitate perception*. If conventional wisdom and perceptual blocks are major hindrances to innovation, then these perception-heightening techniques can be instrumental in enhancing creativity. One example is altering "frame of reference." If you're having trouble finding markets for a new material because you are overwhelmed by its cost—$200 per pound—try telling an outside group that it costs $2.00 per pound and see what happens. You'll get some junk, but you'll get some good applications too. (I know. I did that once.) If you're intimidated by the sheer size of a chemical processing plant that ought to be totally redesigned, try reducing it in your mind (or in the minds of others) to doll-house size. If the components of a circuit are too dinky to work with, scale them up so your designers can see them. Minify. Magnify. Suspend the old laws by engaging in some "what if" thinking. You can come back to reality after you have your new concepts.

Another technique for forcing the perception of a whole is "attribute listing." Here you list all the properties and characteristics of the item you can think of, whether conventionally relevant or not. Attribute listing is especially useful in finding new applications for a product.

Also in this general category is a creative technique called "bionics," which involves seeking analogies in nature for the solution to a problem. A banana is an interesting package. The snapdragon exhibits a possibly useful mechanism for something or other. Maybe the productivity of a back hoe could be significantly increased by incorporating an indexing-daisy design into the business end.

The Design Designers

The third basic category of creative techniques are those *designed to design*. If the essence of creativity is combining known elements into new relationships, then the tools for combining these elements are at the heart of the process. One such tool is a technique called "word mapping." It involves defining and redefining words, beginning with the word that expresses the abstract generalization of the function being considered. For example, if the problem is "What are all the ways I could join the legs to the chair?" you can start with "join" and go from there to "combine," "weld," "meld," "tie," "marry," "screw," "stake," "sweat," "splice." And somewhere along the line, one of the words may stimulate a totally new idea on how to attach the legs to the chair.

Another classic creative technique in this category is "forced relationships," also referred to in the trade as "lateral thinking." It takes the form of a two-column chart. Let's say your objective is to identify new market applications for a standard snap fastener. What you can do is list all the characteristics of a snap in one column. Then, in the next column, list things that are occasionally closed (one of the principal features of a snap).

Snap Characteristics	Occasionally Closed
Pressure-close	Doors
Male/Female	Envelopes
Noise-confirm	Luggage
Tension-open	Bars
Shear strength	Cracker boxes
Fabric plus	Pouches
Positive binary	Blouses
	Bridges
	Minds

Now run your mind over the two columns in any combination and see what suggests itself. A positively closed cracker box that hangs on the side of the liquor cabinet?

You can use other headings for your second column— whatever may have potential. For example, another heading that might be productive for the snap is "Games and Sports." Here you might get a ping-pong ball holder that hangs under the table. You can set up any lists you think might work and then fit them together.

One last example of this type of creative technique is "morphological analysis." Closely related to "lateral thinking," it works like this: You set up your column headings by the constituent components, or areas in which you have decisions to make. Then you generate a number of options in each area separately; finally, you pick and choose from the columns and combine them together to design the whole. An example: Suppose you have to write the script for an episode of a TV serial. OK, get started! What's it going to be this time? Pressure's on! Deadline five o'clock today! What about it?

You haven't a clue, right? You don't know where to start!

Use "morphological analysis." A TV episode has to have a plot—that is, some action. It has to have characters. It has to have a scene or a place to happen. So these are your areas of decision. Set up your columns.

Action	Character	Site
Murder	Cowboy	Elevator
Sex	Little Old Lady	Tavern
Violence	Dog	Graveyard
Racing	Villain	Kitchen
Chase	Siren	Jail
Hiding	Mouse	Desert
Discovery	Parson	Peoria

All you need do now is make your decision—cherry-pick your options—and you practically have your script written. (I make no guarantee as to the reviews you'll get!)

When I was a kid, I used to listen to "The Lone Ranger" on the radio every afternoon at 5:15. That serial went on for years, with Silver and Tonto and miscellaneous characters who entered and exited from time to time. Toward the end of the program's run, the scriptwriters began to go dry on what Kemo-Sabi ought to be doing next. So they resorted to morphological analysis. That's how the Lone Ranger got along in his last days.

Of course, this fundamental creative technique is equally applicable to the specification of the components of complex high-technology systems.

MAKING IT WORK

As emphasized earlier, the leader must "drive" the Innovation Session to make sure it works. "Works" means going in the right direction and making maximum progress.

The leader must withstand the temptation to become immersed in the creative activity, but rather must remain sufficiently aloof to manage the *process*. There may be, for instance, six or seven experts, of diverse backgrounds, participating in the session. There is no distinct, positive correlation between brainpower and, shall we say, volubility. That is to say, some people talk a lot and don't say much; others talk a lot and spew out solid ideas a mile a minute. On the other side, sometimes potentially great contributors are by nature reticent; and some dummies are dummies—they just don't have anything to say.

It is the session leader's responsibility to tune up those who could contribute, leave be those who are contributing to progress, tune down those who are taking up air time without helping the cause, and politely ignore those who have nothing to add and don't peep. After all, it is the leader's responsibility, not to maintain a happy, balanced exchange, but rather to get the goods—to elicit the maximum number of options in and around the target. That's the point. Therefore, the Innovation Session leader will be mainly involved in encouraging and stimulating productive contributions, maintaining pace, and controlling or constraining the timewasters.

This last function must be delicately handled so as not to conflict with the first two functions. That is, the leader—or interlocutor, if you will—must *never* "put down" any member of the group. If he does, he just might kill the spontaneity. He may inhibit those sensitive people who identify with an object of opprobrium. But there are other ways the leader can achieve his objective. Everyone there must observe the rule that positiveness prevails, with respect to both the subject and the interaction between contributors. But the leader has the weapon of "rudeness" at his disposal. He can interrupt with a compliment, use an overpowering voice, utilize body language, stand up, violate "personal space," take control, abruptly redirect the discussion, or throw the ball to a different member of the group. Thus the objective can be accomplished without any observable hostility. Bad manners, perhaps. But no pall will be cast over the group, as would be the case if the leader abruptly drew someone up short.

The Innovation Session leader has a job to do, and he must manage the group dynamics to achieve his ultimate objective.

13

THE BUILDING ON, AND EVALUATION OF, NEW-PRODUCT CONCEPTS

All the companies I've ever had contact with have already recognized their need for new products. But they are usually at either end of a spectrum when it comes to the number of new-product concepts currently available to them. At the one extreme are those companies that are "concept killers." They are very successful in killing any new-product idea, regardless of the source, lest it come to life and threaten the old order. So there they are, without a single new-product possiblity worth talking about.

At the other end of the spectrum are those companies that are "string savers." They never throw anything away. They perpetually collect new-product concepts—good, bad, indifferent. But they never do anything about them. They seem paralyzed by the possibility that if they became enamored of one idea or the other and began actually investing in its development, another, even better idea might come along. And then where would they be?

At both extremes, the need is the same. Companies must establish an orderly process for *building on* any new-product concept that is brought to their attention—modifying and improving the concept, trying to "make it fit"—and then *evaluating* each concept, after it has been worked with, against predetermined benchmarks of what is, and is not, acceptable.

So both the "concept killer" and the "string saver" must do two things *before* evaluating any new-product possibility: (1) establish realistic criteria that describe the minimum characteristics of the ideal new product; and (2) work positively with any new idea suggested, to try to make it meet these criteria.

In addition, the "string saver" must *set aside* all the new-product possibilities it has collected until steps 1 and 2 have been completed. Then, the accumulated concepts may be tested against the criteria, along with any other new ideas suggested.

The cardinal rule of creativity—and the only way to come up, finally, with successful new product lines—is to *suspend judgment*. First, generate all the options you can, in and around the target. Then, and only then, should you evaluate the shots you've fired to see which ones are close enough to the bull's eye to score. Be generative, then evaluative. Fill the hopper first, then cherry-pick the keepers.

The system I've been proposing, the Strategic Innovation Process, includes back to back *two* positive, "hopper filling" efforts: (1) using the best relevant brainpower from the *outside* world (from people knowing everything except the evaluative factors), and (2) using the best brainpower relating to different aspects of the goal from *inside* the company itself. And the third step—evaluation—is also designed to be positive. It involves selecting, by consensus, those concepts that do bear potential, rather than eliminating or damning possible new product lines which, regardless of the effort, will never work.

Throughout the process of generating and evaluating options, there is simply no place for negativism. And when the time does come for judgment, it is *voting*, not vetoing.

After you have collected the best that your outside experts have to offer in the way of suggestions for potential new product lines, your task is to superimpose thereon the best that the *inside* team can offer. The idea is to combine and collate concepts emanating from outside sources for presentation to those who are most familiar with the problem, and who have responsibility for its ultimate solution.

THE BUILDING SESSION

Once you have your ducks in a row, you are in a position to feed the concepts in slowly, in logical sequence, to the inside group, and encourage them to chew on them and build on them, developing the ideas to make them fit their needs.

A word of caution. There are, no doubt, energetic, willing product-development executives among your group of insiders—the group with responsibility for, and complete knowledge of, the problem. However, I believe, emphatically, that it is best to sequester them during the initial concept-generation phase—partly so that they will not inhibit the freewheeling atmosphere of the Innovation Session, and partly so that the concepts themselves can be organized and positioned in such a way that the entire inside team can respond positively and afresh to refining and developing concepts with no name tags on them. If any of your knowledgeable insiders were to be present when an outside expert suggested an idea that had been tried and flopped in 1954—almost bringing about bankruptcy, or almost causing the developer to lose his job—I wouldn't trust that insider not to flinch or start or give some other indication that the idea was perhaps not the best one in the world.

The buffer between outsiders and insiders permits logic to supersede chronology. Related concepts that have come out at different times during the Innovation Session can be grouped together and presented as a part of one general subject area.

It is during this thoughtful-consideration-and-refinement-of-possibilities meeting—I call it the Building Session—that any concepts which may have occurred to people on the inside team can and should be brought out and discussed, along with the new options presented.

How concrete and detailed should these concepts be? And how many should be dealt with at one time?

The answer to the first question is that they should be pretty vague and fuzzy, or at least they should be built up very slowly. For one thing, if any concept is fully engineered and completely market-researched at the time it is first presented, you run great risk of having totally wasted that effort—that is, if the concept does not ultimately "make the cut." (Don't forget that the concepts were initially suggested, for good purpose, by top experts in relevant fields, and that these experts, at the time, "knew the question"—that is, they were properly briefed.)

The other reason relates to NIH. If you introduce a subject area broadly and gradually, it will give the members of the inside team an opportunity to come up with their own new-product concepts in that area. Sometimes, the "creative misconstruction" of an idea winds up being an even better concept. And it certainly doesn't hurt to have it come from the home team!

How many concepts? I'll tell you, there aren't 100 and there aren't 10! I once conducted a Building Session for a client in Boston, following a particularly prolific Innovation Session. There was an awful lot of stuff, and I just doggedly kept plowing through concept after concept: "And here's another interesting idea." The president of the company phoned me the next morning and said, "Please come back and tell us, again, every concept that came after number 40. My guys tuned out at about that point. We were all numb!"

The human brain can operate at high intensity for three to four hours, max. Either you can't deal with as many as 100 ideas during that period, or if you can, you are not doing them justice. So one answer is: less than 100.

Another client, a publisher in New York, told me, "All of those are really in this category, and all of these are simply a different version of _____, and we've actually considered only ten basic business opportunities!"

There is a human tendency to synthesize (and publishers are more human than most of us!). If, during a Building Session, you are collating and fitting different concepts into neat categories, then you are utilizing the left (analytical/propositional) hemisphere of your brain, rather than the right (creative/appositional) hemisphere. And that is also a classic example of failure to perceive fine distinctions (rooted in a number of perfectly normal psychological bascs). So the *other* answer is: whether you know it or not, we've covered more than 40.

SELECTING THE "KEEPERS"

Once you've completed the second "hopper filling" effort, laying out the best ideas from the inside along with the new concepts from outside experts, you are ready for the third stage. It's time to evaluate and select the "keepers" from all those fragile new ideas which have been generated thus far—and which have been allowed to live this long by virtue of the fact that nobody has been permitted to blow any of them out of the water. (That's the rule!)

First, let me assure you that no one expects you to be knowledgeable in businesses that your company is not currently engaged in. Why should you be? Next, let me caution you that the closer to home, the more familiar, a new-product concept is, the "friendlier" it will be—that is, the less threatening or hostile to your "present."

Finally, you should be aware that it is relatively safe to survey, study, and research. That is not threatening. It's easy and rather fun. It is dangerous to take the plunge and actually try something new. And the newer (more different) the idea is, and the closer you are to trying it, the more dangerous it becomes.

So the bottom line is: you are not *qualified* to judge a new concept; you don't *want* to stray very far from home base; and you would *prefer* to study and analyze than to act.

But it must be done. And you and your inside team must do it. It will help if each person understands that he is not trying to get "the" answer at this point. It's a judgment call. There are no facts. It is a matter of opinion as to the potential of each new-product concept to be a winner for your company. And it will help each person to know that he is not alone. Each member of the inside team brings a different background, experience base, and bundle of knowledge to the task.

While everyone is viewing the concepts from a different perspective, all are using the same benchmarks for rating their potential: the ranked criteria, agreed to in advance, that set forth the attributes of the ideal new product.

This is a time for words, not numbers. Some schemes for selection and ranking use numerical weightings. I think that is inadvisable. For one thing, the numbers tend to reduce significantly different concepts to a common denominator. Disparities need to be brought out and discussed intelligently, not obscured. Second, as I pointed out, the situation requires subjective opinions and a "gut feel." In such a case, a hard number tends to be misleading. Numbers are exact; opinions range along a continuum. Unquantifiable intuition is often the best guide.

Besides, on a scale of 1 to 10, if you give me a "3" concept, and a "7" enthusiastic product champion, I'll take my chances any day over the reverse situation.

The In-Situ Delphi System

The process we use in the evaluation and selection stage is called the "in-situ Delphi system."

The original Delphi system was developed about 20 years ago by RAND Corporation for obtaining consensus among experts on forecasts or predictions of future scenarios. It involved sending out open-ended questions to a group of experts by mail; receiving their individual opinions by mail; collating and summarizing all responses to each question; and again sending out the questions, but this time giving each respondent the advantage of knowing his peers' estimates in case he would like to alter his opinion in light of what they thought. The revised opinions are returned by mail, sometimes followed by a second cycle. Finally, the consensus responses to each question are reported.

Lewis Thomas wrote an outstanding piece on the Delphi system in *The New England Journal of Medicine* (February 1976). With his permission, I am including an excerpt of the article here:

> What Delphi is, is a really quiet, thoughtful conversation, in which everyone gets a chance to *listen*. The background noise of small talk, and the recurrent sonic booms of vanity, are eliminated at the outset, and there is time to think. There are no voices, and therefore no rising voices. It is, when you look at it this way, a great discovery. Before Delphi, real listening in a committee meeting had always been a near impossibility. Each member's function was to talk, and while other people were talking the individual member was busy figuring out what he ought to say next, to shore up his own original position. Debating is what committees really do, not thinking. Take away the need for winning points, leading the discussion, protecting one's face, gaining applause, shouting down opposition, scaring opponents, all that kind of noisy activity, and a group of bright people can get down to quiet thought. It is a nice idea, and I'm glad it works.
>
> It is interesting that Delphi is the name chosen, obviously to suggest the oracular prophetic function served. The original Delphi was Apollo's place, and Apollo was the god of prophecy, but more than that. He was also the source of some of the best Greek values: moderation, sanity, care, attention to the rules, deliberation. . . .
>
> Today's Delphi thus represents a refinement of an ancient social device, with a novel modification of committee procedure constraining groups of people to think more quietly, and to listen. The method seems new, as a formal procedure, but it is really very old, perhaps as old as human society itself. For in real life, this is the way we've always arrived at decisions, even though it has always been done in a disorganized way. We pass the word around; we ponder how the case is put by different people; we read the poetry; we meditate over the literature; we play the music; we change our minds; we reach an understanding. Society evolves this way, not by shouting each other down, but by the unique capacity of unique, individual human beings to comprehend each other.

The basic Delphi technique has a lot of good in it. The only trouble is that in the real world few of us have time to wait for the mails. We've got to get the decision and get moving. But that's all right. We can do it on the spot ("in situ," as it were) and still preserve the benefits of the Delphi system. Here's how it works.

1. Number all your new-product concepts (which should have been recorded on flip charts) in the order they were presented and developed.

2. Ask each member of the team to take a sheet of paper, lay out three vertical columns headed "A," "B," and "C," and put his initials on the paper.

3. Explain what each heading signifies: "A" means "Appears to me to have potential for meeting the main criteria for a successful new product for us"; "C" means "Will never fly"; "B" means "I don't know" and is reserved for any concept that does not fit (in the opinion of that individual) into column A or column C.

4. Direct the team's attention to each concept, in sequence, reading it as it was recorded and amplifying it if necessary. Ask that each member of the team place the concept number in one of the three columns. (That forces a decision on each concept: yes, no, or maybe. It is a hip shot. Everybody can handle it.)

5. After this secret ballot, call for the "A" votes of each member of the team individually, and post them by the concepts in full view of everyone. It doesn't matter who you start with or how you proceed, except that the senior executive on the team should be called on last. The idea is to avoid cross-contamination of opinion at the outset. (I have found that some concepts always get unanimous "A" votes, some concepts get a few "A" votes, and some concepts get none.)

6. Start the process of negotiation. The clear winners do not require a lot of discussion; the clear losers can't be saved because they have no advocate. It is the ones in the middle that are the subject of legitimate debate—those that some members of the team feel have potential for meeting the essential criteria, and that others either believe to be losers or don't know.

It is in this last step that the in-situ Delphi system improves on the original. Because here, on the spot, any member of the team can take the floor and eloquently plead for his favorite. It may well be the case (and often is) that he possesses certain information that others do not have which leads him to an opposite conclusion. It is quite possible that the VP of marketing knows something that the VP of R&D does not, and vice versa. When this knowledge is shared, everybody has the opportunity to make a decision grounded on the same basis (that led at least one individual to form a positive opinion). One expert may persuade his peers to come over to his way of thinking.

Gaining the real-time reaction of the group is a major benefit of the in-situ Delphi system. This is especially important for the "string saver" company or for the "persistent promoter" within an organization. Have you ever experienced the situation in which a person plumps for his favorite idea for years, until it becomes a company joke (to all but him)? Nothing seems to be able to turn him away. Well, with the in-situ Delphi system, he finally has his day in court. He has the podium, with all the powers-that-be giving him a fair opportunity to sell his idea, once and for all. If he succeeds, he wins the budget necessary to develop it; if he fails, then the idea is finally killed and he is convinced it simply will never be supported, at least in this company.

The result of the in-situ Delphi exercise will be a few winners, a few survivors out of all the candidates considered. And the beauty of it is you have killed the turkeys on the spot. You'll never hear about the losers again. To paraphrase W. C. Fields, new-product concepts are like kittens: you've got to drown them before you get attached to them. The in-situ Delphi system is the means for doing that.

On the positive side, out of the 40 or so possible new-product concepts that the team considers, 4 to 8 may survive. The actual number depends on the ease of the task (that is, the reasonableness of the criteria), the quality of the concepts themselves, and the team's degree of positiveness.

A word on battle losing, war winning, and perspicacity. Remember the "3" idea and the "7" champion? That could be what you've got! And how do you know, anyway, what will and will not succeed in the future? For a successful business venture, you don't need *everybody* on the team; you don't even need a majority. All you need is one strong champion. And all he needs is support from the top. Top management's job is to prevent organized opposition to the development of the idea from within the organization. And the champion just might come through with a new business for the corporation!

PART THREE

IMPLEMENTING ACTION

14

ORCHESTRATING NEW-PRODUCT DEVELOPMENT AND MARKET RESEARCH

Management sage Peter Drucker has said: "Every great idea ultimately degenerates into hardware." After you come up with all the great ideas you can, and after they are evaluated and the best of the lot are selected, the time comes when you have to stop studying and creating and planning—and go *do* something. Time for action!

Presumably, at this point, you have a number of new-product concepts at hand, any one of which may possess the potential to be a resounding success in the marketplace, and a magnificently profitable future product line for your company. But it's a long way from here to there. The hard work is just starting. So who within your organization is to be responsible for bringing victory home? For shoe-horning one of these "nothing" concepts through the line to the end goal—a product that your company will ultimately manufacture and sell profitably?

Just as the Army is marvelously staffed, trained, and equipped to fight the *last* war, so your organization may be ideally equipped and staffed to develop your *last* new product. But what about your next winner? It is not going to be the same.

CHOOSING A PILOT

In his book *On the Psychology of Military Incompetence*, Norman Dixon argues that the very characteristics needed for successful leadership in war—ability to tolerate uncertainty, spontaneity of thought and action, open-mindedness—are the antithesis of the personality traits needed to meet the requirements of military life and to attract recruits in the first place—obedience, orderliness, fear of failure, need for approval. The system makes little allowance for innovation, initiative, and independent thought. Does that situation bear any resemblance to the capacity of your organization, as is, to develop your next new product?

Again, the main question is: Who within your company will take the responsibility and do the job? Committees don't really *do* anything; they review and approve (or, more likely, scrub) proposals. They are a convenient device for diluting or avoiding responsibility. We are looking for the *pilot*—the real-time, hands-on, decision-making, self-committing hero. You're seeking an individual, and a special kind of individual, at that.

You can recruit him from inside the organization or outside the organization—those are the only two possible places he could come from. In the latter case, you may opt for a heavyweight in the field you intend to penetrate. He really knows his way around in this market, which is alien to you, because you've never been there. Trouble is, he knows nothing about the policies and folkways of your particular company. You'll have to bring him up to speed and integrate him into your organization.

The other choice is to select someone from within your organization, who is fully familiar with how to get things done internally, and in whom you have complete confidence—and he knows nothing, for starters, about the field you are about to enter.

I don't think there is a general answer. They both work. It depends on which is the more crucial to success—outside knowledge or inside knowledge.

In any case, you want someone with a derring-do, entre-preneurial spirit. Avoid those made ordinary by having done the same thing repeatedly and reliably over a long period of time. Pass over the "maintenance manager" who has earned a track record in a narrow discipline. Eliminate from consideration the stable conformist who never departed from convention, never shattered an icon. In the process of new-product development, you win no points for "following standard procedures": losers as well as winners can follow all the rules!

Once you select your pilot, give him an airplane, a clear char-ter, and a budget to get the job done. Next, remove the landing gear from his airplane so that there's no way he can land if his mission does not succeed. Now or never. Job on the line.

A chicken and a pig were strolling by a diner one morning and the chicken smiled and said, "Isn't it nice—doesn't it make you feel proud—that we are responsible, you and I, for enabling those humans to enjoy their breakfast?" The pig replied, "That's easy for you to say. For you it's merely a contribution. For me it's a total commitment!"

You have to put your pilot in the pig's position. All or nothing, no place to hide, do or die. New-product development is hard and dangerous work. It can't (or will not) be handled off the side of the desk of someone with other (safer) responsibilities. It re-quires total commitment. Reward for success, commensurate, of course. For high-rollers, it is a good, visible, fast route to the top.

The responsibility for success lies with the pilot. That respon-sibility has been assigned him by the chairman, or CEO, or who-ever bears ultimate responsibility for the future growth of the company. New-product development is that important.

The problem is the pilot will need a good deal of help and cooperation from others in the organization. Generally, within the typical corporation, the amount of "help and cooperation" accorded an executive is related to his perceived power, and there is a direct, positive correlation between the two. The more power, the more cooperation. It is a fact of life that an executive's "natural" perceived power is a function of the size of his fiefdom—measured in terms of the dollars accounted for by his unit or the number of employees that have a solid-line reporting relationship to him.

The pilot may have nothing but dotted lines beneath him and beside him, and he probably has authority over zero dollars of *current* income-producing activity. Solution: The CEO must *provide* the pilot with what is called "nominal" power. That is, he must give him clear authority to command the kind of cooperation he needs to get the job done. The CEO must support his new-product development pilot and must come out of the closet and give visibility to his support—wholeheartedly, staunch, unflagging, confident. The pilot needs to have a clear mandate to wield the power of the chief executive officer in the eyes of those from whom he needs cooperation. That's the only way the job will get done.

What is this "job"? It's very simple, or should be very simple. You've got to *keep* it simple. Otherwise, the corporation runs the risk of overcomplicating and overspending on what should be, at least initially, a quick-shot "fly-by." You've got to stay light on your feet. Follow trails, have a quick look-see, check it out.

THE THREE-POINT CHECK

There are only three things that must be done at this point—two simultaneously, and one thereafter: (1) check out the produceability of the product by your company; (2) do the necessary market research; then (3) run the numbers.

Numbers

Let me deal with the third thing first. A firm in Switzerland is anxious to know whether to manufacture and market in the United States a new product it is considering. We just received a cable from the company advising us that it is at the point of doing an economic analysis, and asking us to supply information on the price the company should assume the product can be sold at, and an estimate of volume of production. At this writing, I am still wrestling with what our response should be, inasmuch as the market research is only part-way completed and the company does not as yet, therefore, have the feedback necessary to make decisions regarding how the product should be designed and marketed.

The Swiss firm got one thing right, however: combining the subjects of price and volume. You can't really separate the two. You can't ask a question about what price you should sell a new product for without making an assumption as to volume; and you can't ask how many units you can sell without knowing what price you're talking about. Basic supply–demand economics dictates the relationship: the higher the price, the less you sell; the lower the price, the more you sell. Costs and production volume face the same immutable law, for a different reason. (Of course, there are exceptions. With perfume, for example, you can sell more if you raise the price. One company I know manufactures products that have gained a reputation for being of higher quality than competing products. The company recently raised the price of a new product, following introduction, and found that it sold much better!) In any case, the principle stands—you have to consider price and quantity together.

The main point is that the financial analysis must come *after* the determination of the market for a new product (how sold, to whom, for what price), and *after* the determination of the design configuration and quality level to which it will be produced. Only then can you grind in your discounted-cash-flow assumptions and begin playing what-if games.

Market and Technical Investigation

Now for the first two (simultaneous) steps: the produceability check and the market research on any and all of the potential new-product candidates you have at hand. It is well if you have several that you can start down the road at once. That way, you are sure to come up with a winner, or even a choice of winners, rather than keeping a turkey alive that should be killed simply because you have nothing else to develop.

Reproduced in Figure 7 is what I call the "Landvater Snail," a graph that depicts the sequence of events in checking out a new-product concept. It was published in *Planned Innovation* (March–April 1980), in an article reporting on a seminar that John Landvater conducted in London. Mr. Landvater is one of the world's leading experts in bringing a new product from the concept stage through to market introduction.

I was with John Landvater in May 1980 in Chicago and we discussed his "Snail" at length. He agreed that the technical research and market investigation should proceed simultaneously. Pressed as to which should come first, if you had to make a choice (which you usually don't), he suggested—and I agreed—that the market research should precede the technical investigation. So reverse, in your mind, "market" and "technical" in Figure 7. It is foolish to find a great market for a product you can't produce, but

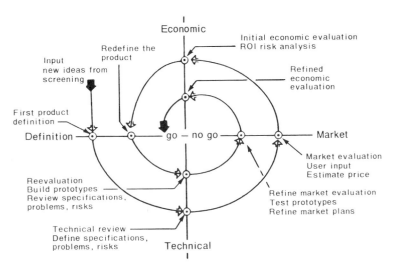

Figure 7. Sequence of procedures in a product feasibility study.

it's even more foolish to tie down all the design tolerances for a product that you'd love to manufacture but nobody wants to buy! This calls up the time-honored question: Which came first, the chicken or the egg? (The answer, of course, is that the egg came first. A chicken is simply the egg's way of making another egg.)

One major corporation in the health and beauty-aid (HBA) industry follows this basic procedure for screening concepts:

> Product concepts would be developed for those ideas which appear to have high feasibility. These concepts would then be exposed to consumers in focus groups to determine the extent of interest. The most promising ideas would then proceed to quantified concept test (QCT).
>
> Detailed R&D evaluations would then be conducted for those ideas which perform well in QCT to determine costs and timing to bring a product to market.
>
> Development programs would be initiated for those product(s) which have the greatest potential for near-term development at a reasonable cost.

I asked one of the company's executives which step is done first, as a rule. She replied that they always check the market first and then do the manufacturing feasibility investigation only on the survivors—except for a few "notable exceptions."

That's to be expected of HBA concerns. They are especially market-oriented in their outlook. And the principal asset of such companies is their brand—their reputation in the marketplace. So if they discover a market need for a new product in the health and beauty-aid field that fits their name and position, they may well go ahead with it, regardless—even if they have to subcontract its manufacture.

The PERT Chart

Another way to express this dual, simultaneous chore graphically is by a PERT chart, as shown in Figure 8. A PERT schedule is appropriate because the two streams—marketing and technical—must interact; and the new-product concept often changes or undergoes a metamorphosis as it goes down each

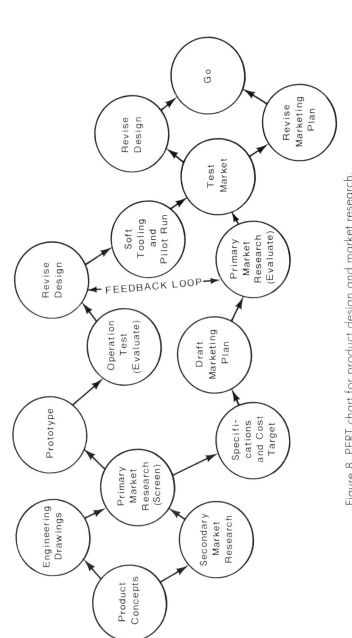

Figure 8. PERT chart for product design and market research.

stream. That is, you *expect* change; you *seek* to develop the new-product concept as you examine its marketability and as you investigate its produceability. And the twists and turns in one area will have impact on the other area.

One advantage of a PERT chart is that it clearly shows the dependency relationships among "events." That is, it forces you to await the result of one activity before proceeding with another activity which should reflect and be built upon that result. The other main advantage of the PERT chart is that it nails down the schedule for each event in advance. That prevents a new-product concept from languishing in the research department, to be tinkered with ad infinitum.

Let's imagine you conceived a new gas-mixing/regulator device that may have application in the operating room and in the welding shop. From the market you discover it "wants" to be green. From the test lab you determine that it has a maximum throughput capacity of 100 CFS. Now, you have to build in a feedback loop—to see if the shop can make it green and if the market will tolerate a 100 CFS upper limit.

From this simple example, we draw three conclusions:

1. (*Again.*) You ought to investigate market and produce-ability concurrently, not serially.

2. Flexibility is the watchword. You don't earn any medals for coming back with the same concept you went out with. The concept you start with should be looked on as a seed idea—a seed from which you hope to make something grow, even though you haven't the faintest notion what the flower will look like. It is most unlikely that the raw concept, in exactly its original form, will end up being the final version that finds its place in the market and is ultimately manufactured on the production floor. You are taking the concept out to allow the marketplace—and the test lab—to redesign your product for you. You are not asking the binary question, "Will it or won't it?" "Can I or can't I?" Rather, you are asking "What?" and "How?"

3. You've got to build in feedback loops—change checkpoints—between these concurrent activities so that you can make

progress in developing a final product that you can both make and sell!

Keep in mind that the "technical investigative unit" of any organization is always, and will always be, 100 percent loaded with work. Whether it's called the research department, research and development division, or test lab, that group is completely and totally busy, and has been since the day it was formed. And as soon as a new scientist or development engineer comes on board, he will have no "time available" from the day he reports to work. It's a classic manifestation of Parkinson's First.

There is a company in the Midwest that manufactures small kitchen appliances. The tempo of its new-product development activity is very high, understandably. The company has had some winners, and some losers. I asked the president why the company did not develop a hot-air popcorn popper. He replied that the R&D department was completely loaded at the time. I did not pursue the question. You have to wonder if R&D was busy developing some products that were less successful than the popcorn popper that Christmas.

Point is, top management must constantly review *what* is being worked on and *how long* each project is being worked on in the research lab. There is a natural tendency to work on an existing project instead of a new one—regardless of the relative, objective benefit of doing more development (as contrasted with initiating development) in any situation requiring the establishment of priorities. Bottom line: top management (to whom the marketing department also reports) must continually review priorities for R&D effort.

So much for "technical." Now for "market." The watchwords are *optimism* and *perseverance.* You've got to go out with a positive, optimistic attitude, confident that you can carve out a niche somewhere for your new-product concept. Anybody with a new idea is always, in the beginning, a minority of one. And he faces a world full of people with vested interests—pride in their current position in the market, desire for the security of status quo, and

Machiavellian hostility toward anything new. Fortunately, the market researcher can also find people who are alert, perceptive, aggressive, and open to new possibilities.

With a negative attitude, it is easy to build a case that *any* new idea is "bad." With a positive attitude, you can *force* your new idea into a world that up to now had no ready-made place for it. You must *project* potential markets in situations where there is no direct base of comparison (because your new-product concept is, after all, new).

Perseverance. The answers rarely fall into your lap, but sometimes it's even worse than that. I have talked to a lot of people in an "industry" and obtained nothing but general, conflicting, mushy opinions and information that somehow did not seem to be on the mark. Then finally we stumbled onto an obscure subsegment of the "industry" where, at last, everything fell into place.

In another instance I talked to the chief engineer in every leading firm in the "industry" and could not succeed in raising a glimmer of interest. Finally, as I dropped to the second and third tier below the leaders, I contacted a hard-charging vice president of engineering in a small but aggressive firm in that industry. He seized upon the new-product concept and agreed to run with it (contract to purchase the initial lot) in order to achieve an edge on his laconic, conservative competitors. I have about concluded that there is no such thing as an "industry"—only a number of firms doing roughly the same thing in different ways, and with different positions and different philosophies of doing business. So you can use SIC codes for starters, OK, but never forget that they were devised by the federal government to keep records of past events. You've got to keep digging, in any field where you think you might hit paydirt!

Finally, remember there are limits. With some new-product concepts, there comes a time when the cord should be pulled. They've had their chance and they just can't make it. If a new-product concept begins to trot like a turkey, gobble like a turkey, and look like a turkey, it may be a turkey! Killing turkeys is top management's job.

That's the beauty of starting out with several new-product concepts for the first-round "fly-by" on the Landvater Snail. You can kill a lot of turkeys and prevent the company from spending *real* money developing them part way. At the same time, you obtain insurance on the survivors. When it comes time to invest in them, you can have confidence that they are winners.

15

THE BENEFITS OF
THE STRATEGIC
INNOVATION PROCESS

For the process of new-product development to be carried out productively by any firm—industrial-product or consumer-product based; technically oriented or market oriented; supplying a product or a service or something in between—the principles underlying the Strategic Innovation Process *must* be applied, and the tenets set forth *must* be observed. Nothing else works!

No reason you can't modify the specifics—you *should* tailor the basic approaches and precepts to suit your particular circumstances. But, in any case, you simply have to follow the Strategic Innovation Process in order to maximize the productivity of your new-product development program.

"Productivity," as I am defining it here, means "getting the biggest bang for the buck" in coming up with new products for your company. In other words, the result of the effort must be *surely* successful, and you have to end up with at least one profitable new product line. Further, you must achieve that objective at the lowest possible cost in terms of resources brought to bear on the task. (Almost by definition, that also implies that you get through in the shortest possible time.) As pointed out earlier, there are some advantages to having the process handled by a skilled third-party outsider, but I want to emphasize the viability of the Strategic Innovation System (or analogs, or basic parts, thereof) in the hands of an in-house "pilot." That works. It is proved by the success of individual executives who have been tutored in the process—in Presidents Association seminars (special programs conducted by the American Management Associations) and other symposia—and who have gone out and *done* it! Sometimes, the Strategic Innovation System is run by an "insider" who reports to the CEO and operates *pro tem* as an arm's-length, pseudo outsider—with a mission.

Here are the main advantages, and the by-products, of the system. (The ancillary benefits should not be discounted.)

1. It widens your company's available resources. You are tapping the world's top expertise through the most knowledgeable individuals in fields that are foreign to you and yet most relevant to your company's goals. There's no way you could hire this caliber and diversity of talent, and you wouldn't want to, anyway. All you need is their input at the leading edge.

2. It forces the merger of the best that the outside world can offer with the best that the company can muster, and concentrates those "bests" on the difficult taks of successful new-product development.

3. It is a means of attracting the attention of the top shooters of the company to a future-oriented task that would otherwise be relegated to a side-stream position and, at best (if ever), receive left-handed, occasional, uncoordinated effort. It provides the staff functionary—the director of new-product development— with real clout. It serves to put the importance (in the long run) of new-product development into the proper perspective within the whole of ongoing operations.

4. There is some value—it is confirmed more often than not—in simply getting all the top functional managers of the

organization together in one place at once, talking about one subject. How many times does that happen? Probably not at all. The system provides a legitimate opportunity for executives with different values, backgrounds, and perspectives to exchange views and take positions on a single subject. The process earns its stripes as a "communications device," alone, to the betterment of the organization.

5. Within the context of the conventional business environment, the process permits and encourages (and indeed requires) behavior that is calculated to result in innovative thought. In effect, you have the opportunity to suspend the protocol of routine maintenance of ongoing operations, for a legitimate long-run purpose. The "rules" don't apply temporarily and selectively here.

6. The mere existence of an organized, planned program, in and of itself, will make new-product development happen. The discipline of a schedule for the reporting of progress forces progress.

7. The discipline of requiring specific tasks to be accomplished in sequence, rather than a mongrelized assault on a vague objective, hoping for an opportunistic hit, ensures an orderly, productive, workmanlike approach to new-product development.

8. The Strategic Innovation Process, while qualitative in nature, is quantitative in approach. A large number of options are purposely generated. These beginning concepts can then be modified, as dictated by the realities of the market and the capabilities of the producing firm. A good number of them may also be scrubbed, without adverse effect on the end goal. And all of this takes place under "laboratory conditions," enabling rigid control of initial costs. Essentially, all concepts are on equal footing until they can prove themselves, and no one concept can attain the status of an authorized, funded project purely on the basis of the persuasiveness of its sponsor.

9. The system is very similar to an insurance policy: it has a known present cost, willingly incurred to avert an unknown fu-

ture disaster. When I enlisted, some years ago, the U.S. Air Force tried to figure out what to do with me. They tentatively decided to attach me to the U.S. Army, long enough to teach me the Russian language at Army Language School in Monterey. But first they sent me to an intensive "prelanguage" course of their own, along with a hundred other candidates, in an attempt to "wash out" early those who would not ultimately survive. The big expenses of training, like the big costs of new-product development, are *downstream*. If the system did nothing but kill concepts, it would be worth it!

10. The positive side of the coin: several firms I have dealt with have, going in, had more new-product concepts than they knew what to do with. More accurately, they did not have sufficient confidence in any one, to the exclusion of the others, to make the investment decision necessary to develop and introduce a new product line. By formalizing the competition and allowing the best new concepts from outside experts to take their place alongside preexisting ideas, the process helps to convince management decision makers. That is, they acquire sufficient confidence in the winners to bite the bullet and "go for it" with one or more of the survivors.

11. Going through the process once will turn up a *number* of viable new-product concepts, not just one. So the company may choose which one of several to develop and introduce first. And the others—those with red ribbons—go in the company's bank of "next new products," to be developed later (unless, of course, a competitor beats you to the concept when its time has come).

12. Just going through the Strategic Innovation Process will provide lasting, general benefits to any organization. Top executives will gain an understanding and appreciation of creative techniques (which they can employ for other purposes as well). They will acquire a license, from time to time, to behave and think differently from your typical hat-wearing, old-money executive from Pittsburgh. Finally, the participants should develop a new level of friendship, an esprit de corps.

SELECTED READINGS

This reading list was prepared by George B. Davies of Riseley, Bedford, England. Mr. Davies is an outstanding professional in the field of creativity. It is reprinted here with his permission.

Adams. J. L. *Conceptual Blockbusting*. San Francisco: W. H. Freeman & Co., 1974.

Adams examines aspects of thinking that are essential for improving our conceptual abilities but that are often underemphasized in our education. The book offers exercises for identifying and overcoming many mental blocks to creativity.

Campbell, D. P. *Take the Road to Creativity and Get Off Your Dead End*, Niles, Ill.: Argus Communications, 1977.

With an enthusiastic personal style, Campbell presents creativity as a rewarding part of an active life. There are chapters on the nature of creativity, characteristics of creative people, family and organizational influence on creativity, and the importance of a risk-taking spirit—all presented in an interest-holding collage of advice, description, anecdotes, puzzles, exercises, and upbeat graphics.

de Bono, E. *Lateral Thinking for Management*. New York: McGraw-Hill, 1972.

One of the most prolific writers on the topic of creativity, de Bono coined the term "lateral thinking." In this book he forges a number of useful links between creativity and management.

de Bono, E. *Opportunities: A Handbook of Business Opportunity Search*. London: Associated Business Programmes, 1978.

In this handbook de Bono explores a number of aspects of "opportunity search," including people motivation, corporate structure, and the methodology of discovering opportunities.

Gordon, W. J. J. *Synectics*. New York: Collier Books, 1961.

The Synectics approach to problem solving is based on the hypothesis that the irrational and emotional are more important to the creative process than the intellectual and rational. Gordon describes his research and discusses the psychological theories supporting the Synectics technique.

Gryskiewicz, S.S. *Targeted Innovation: A Situational Approach*. Greensboro, N.C.: Proceedings of Creativity Week III, Center for Creative Leadership, 1980.

After analyzing some of the factors that can inhibit creativity and innovation, Gryskiewicz presents a model that attempts to match the type of problem to the type of person and the particular creative technique to be used in order to achieve maximum effectiveness.

Kepner, C. H., and Trego, B. B. *The Rational Manager*. New York: McGraw-Hill, 1965.

This eminently readable and practical book helps the manager improve his or her problem-solving and decision-making ability by the efficient use of information. The authors present a decision-making model that is particularly useful for idea sorting.

MacKinnon, D.W. *In Search of Human Effectiveness: Identifying and Developing Creativity*. Buffalo, N.Y.: Creative Education Foundation, 1978.

This publication brings together MacKinnon's vast background in the nature and nurture of creativity. It should be of interest to teachers, managers, parents, and all who are concerned with the creative development of themselves and others.

Parnes, S. J., and Harding, H. F. A *Source Book for Creative Thinking*. New York: Charles Scribner's Sons, 1962.

Despite its "age," this book provides an excellent overview of the subject of creativity.

Prince, G. *The Practice of Creativity*. New York: Harper & Row, 1970.

Prince worked with W. J. J. Gordon in the development of Synectics. His book provides detailed descriptions of the rules, roles, and mechanisms of the Synectics problem-solving technique, along with excerpts from successful Synectics sessions.

Van Gundy, A. B. *Techniques of Structured Problem Solving*. London: Van Nostrand Reinhold Co. Ltd., 1981.

Seventy individual and group techniques are featured in this book. Each technique is followed by an evaluation of its particular strengths and weaknesses. Decision flowcharts and guidelines are included to assist in choosing techniques for various problem-solving stages.

INDEX